PRACTICE
MAKES
PERFECT

Italian
Pronouns &
Prepositions

Daniela Gobetti

McGraw·Hill

New York   Chicago   San Francisco   Lisbon   London   Madrid   Mexico City
Milan   New Delhi   San Juan   Seoul   Singapore   Sydney   Toronto

1 2 3 4 5 6 7 8 9 0   VLP/VLP   2 1 0 9 8 7 6

ISBN 0-07-145393-8
Library of Congress Control Number: 2005931313

McGraw-Hill books are available at special quantity discounts to use as premiums and sales promotions, or for use in corporate training programs. For more information, please write to the Director of Special Sales, Professional Publishing, McGraw-Hill, Two Penn Plaza, New York, NY 10121-2298. Or contact your local bookstore.

This book is printed on acid-free paper.

Contents

Preface

This book is intended to help beginning and intermediate students of Italian to achieve proficiency in using pronouns and prepositions. Italian pronouns are complex. They are an excellent illustration of the fact that Italian derives historically from Latin, which is a highly inflected language. Achieving competence in the use of Italian pronouns is therefore not easy. Yet, pronouns come early in the learning process, as soon as the speaker wishes to move beyond utterly elementary sentences, and as soon as the reader wishes to comprehend a text of even limited complexity. Prepositions are notoriously difficult to learn in every language. They contribute to possible meanings of groups of words: even the incomplete phrase "with my brother" creates altogether different expectations from the phrase "by my brother." But by themselves, in most cases, prepositions merely link words to convey meaning. Prepositions therefore sound (and are) arbitrary to non-native speakers; only prolonged practice can make people feel comfortable using them.

This book aims to be true to its title: *Practice Makes Perfect*. It provides the essential grammatical rules necessary for use of a pronoun or a preposition. It also provides as many exercises as possible, using repetition and variation on patterns as its main pedagogical tools. The book assumes that students will learn to contextualize phrases and sentences in their classes, or through other self-instruction books, and helps students develop semiautomatic responses to the association of one word with another: «**Si** lava le mani» means "He/she washes **his/her** hands." «**Le** lavo le mani» can only mean "I'm washing **her** hands." The first part of the book is devoted to pronouns, the second to prepositions. Readers may choose to use only the latter and not the former, or to invert the order. The book was written, however, starting from the assumption that there is a logical progression from pronouns to prepositions; after all, we often encounter pronouns that need no prepositions. On the other hand, prepositions can be applied to various parts of speech, including pronouns. Grammatical points explained in Part I are assumed to have been learned by the time the user begins Part II. Exercises vary in difficulty from beginning to intermediate. Complexity of grammatical points, and of the vocabulary and grammatical structures used in the exercises, will alert users to the degree of difficulty of each exercise. Beginning exercises require knowledge of the simple present of the indicative and of the imperative, the gerund, and the infinitive. When a different tense or mode are necessary even in simple sentences, they have been provided in parentheses. However, a few beginning exercises have been included that require knowledge of the passive voice. As far as possible, all phrases and sentences in the exercises that require translation (Italian into English or vice versa) can be translated literally. When an idiomatic expression was indispensable, I added its translation in parentheses. *Practice Makes Perfect* is for self-study learners and students working with instructors. There are cases when more than one translation will be correct, even though only one has been provided.

I wish to thank Gino Balducci, Silvia Giorgini, and my husband, Michael Bonner, for their useful suggestions.

Mi auguro che questo libro vi aiuti a imparare i pronomi e le preposizioni rapidamente e senza fare (troppa) fatica.

PART I

PRONOUNS

In general, pronouns allow us to point to or mention someone or something without naming them directly. They enable us to convey qualitative and quantitative features of persons and things and to link main and dependent clauses by referring to something that is contained in the preceding sentence.

Even though pronouns often replace nouns or names mentioned before, they do not always do so: *I* and *you*, for example, do not require any antecedent. We use them to refer to people who are present while we are talking about and with them.

These general features hold for both Italian and English, as does the overall classification of pronouns: *subject pronouns* (*I, you, he, she,* etc.); *object pronouns* (*me, you, him, her,* etc.); and *relative pronouns* (*who, whose, whom,* etc.). There are some differences, but none significant enough to prevent students from following the structure of this book, which adopts the classification as we find it in Italian. Appendix 1 summarizes the pronouns covered in this book.

The most significant differences between English and Italian are:

Italian pronouns vary in person, gender, and number more than English pronouns do. Possessive pronouns, for example, take four forms: **il mio, la mia, i miei, le mie**, which all translate the English pronoun *mine*.

In Italian there are a greater variety and number of pronouns, each of which plays a specific function: **lui** means *he*; **lui/lo** mean *him*; **gli** means *to him*; **si** translates as *himself*; and so on.

In order to become proficient in the use of Italian pronouns, students need a basic understanding of gender and number options and of principles of coordination among pronouns, nouns, adjectives, verbs, etc.—and they will need a lot of practice, which the exercises in this book are intended to provide.

Subject Pronouns

Subject pronouns usually replace a noun that has already been mentioned (the antecedent). At times the antecedent noun is understood: the pronoun *I* refers to the speaker, and the pronoun *you* refers to the person to whom the speaker is talking.

Pronouns and Conjugations

There are six basic *persons* (**persone**) in both Italian and English: first, second, and third person singular; first, second, and third person plural. They are not capitalized, unless they follow a punctuation mark that requires the next word to be capitalized.

io, tu, lui/lei, noi, voi, loro (*I, you, he/she, we, you, they*)

In Italian, verb forms usually vary in all persons. Here follows an example of regular verbs from the first, second, and third conjugations in the present indicative.

amare (*to love*)		temere (*to fear*)		sentire (*to hear*)	
io amo	I love	**io temo**	I fear	**io sento**	I hear
tu ami	you love	**tu temi**	you fear	**tu senti**	you hear
lui/lei ama	he/she loves	**lui/lei teme**	he/she fears	**lui/lei sente**	he/she hears
noi amiamo	we love	**noi temiamo**	we fear	**noi sentiamo**	we hear
voi amate	you love	**voi temete**	you fear	**voi sentite**	you hear
loro amano	they love	**loro temono**	they fear	**loro sentono**	they hear

esercizio   1-1

Match the subject pronouns listed on the left with their appropriate verb forms.

_____ 1. io   a. canta

_____ 2. voi   b. cantano

_____ 3. lui   c. canto

_____ 4. noi   d. canti

_____ 5. tu   e. cantiamo

_____ 6. loro   f. cantate

esercizio   1-2

Match the subject pronouns listed on the left with their appropriate verb forms.

_____ 1. voi   a. balli

_____ 2. io   b. pagano

_____ 3. lui   c. pensiamo

_____ 4. tu   d. osservo

_____ 5. noi   e. comprate

_____ 6. loro   f. gioca

The Third Person Singular and Plural

In Italian, the first and second person singular and plural have only one form each: **io, tu, noi, voi** (*I, you, we, you*). English uses *you*, which conveys both the second person plural and the second person singular. The third person can take different forms.

Forms of the third person

Singular	**egli/lui**	he
	ella/lei	she
	 **esso/essa**	it
Plural	**essi/esse/loro**	they

Italian uses different forms of the third person singular and plural for people, animals, and things, as illustrated in the following table.

Third person singular and plural

HUMAN BEINGS	HOUSEHOLD PETS	ANIMALS	THINGS
egli/lui/ella/lei	**lui/lei**	**esso/essa/lui/lei**	**esso/essa**
essi/esse/loro	**loro**	**essi/esse/loro**	**essi/esse**

The pronouns **egli/ella** are rarely used in everyday language, either written or spoken. **Lui/lei/loro** are now used for both people and animals, especially household pets. **Esso/essa/essi/esse** are used for things. Throughout this book, the more colloquial forms **lui/lei** and **loro** are used.

Lei ha scritto un libro bellissimo.	**She** *wrote a very beautiful book.*
Lui sembra feroce, invece è un cane dolcissimo.	**He** *looks fierce, but in fact he's a very sweet dog.*
Loro sono proprio degli sciocchi!	**They** *are such fools!*

Italian uses subject pronouns less than English, because other words in the sentence convey the agent: the verb conveys the *person* (and therefore the *number*); past participles, adjectives, and nouns used as qualifiers may convey *gender* and *number* as well. When we are uncertain about the gender of the person/people we are talking about, or when a group includes males and females, qualifiers take the masculine.

È **contento** (*masc. sing.*).	**He's** *happy.*
È **contenta** (*fem. sing.*).	**She's** *happy.*
Sono **contenti** (*masc. pl.*).	**They're** *happy.*
Sono **contente** (*fem. pl.*).	**They're** *happy.*
Quando sei **partito** (*masc. sing.*)?	*When did* **you** *leave?*
Quando siete **partite** (*fem. pl.*)?	*When did* **you** *leave?*
Siamo **andati** al bar (*masc. pl.*).	**We** *went to the bar.*
Sono delle **brave maestre** (*fem. pl.*).	**They** *are good teachers.*

esercizio | **1-3**

Match the pronouns in the column on the left with the appropriate sentence on the right, choosing among **io, tu, lui, lei, esso/essa, noi, voi, essi/esse, loro.** *(The words in parentheses give clues to the gender of the subject.)*

_____ 1. lei   a. bevo il caffé.

_____ 2. voi   b. amano giocare. (*le foche*)

_____ 3. io   c. hanno vinto. (*i nostri avversari*)

_____ 4. essi   d. comprate il gelato.

_____ 5. noi   e. parli al telefono.

_____ 6. loro   f. è contenta.

_____ 7. tu   g. sono mammiferi. (*i pipistrelli*)

_____ 8. esso   h. è sempre stanco.

_____ 9. esse   i. andiamo al mare.

_____ 10. lui   j. è alto. (*il grattacielo*)

esercizio   1-4

Insert the appropriate pronouns, choosing among **io, tu, lui, lei, esso/essa, noi, voi, essi/esse, loro**. (The words in parentheses give clues to the gender of the subject.)

1. _____ rido.

2. _____ paghiamo.

3. _____ sciano.

4. _____ corri.

5. _____ studia. (*mio fratello*)

6. _____ abbaia. (*il cane dei vicini*)

7. _____ vede. (*Lucia*)

8. _____ sentite.

9. _____ capiamo.

10. _____ mangiano il miele. (*gli orsi*)

esercizio   1-5

Choose the appropriate form of the verb shown in parentheses to match the subject of the following sentences. Use the simple present tense of the indicative.

1. Lui _____ molto ogni notte. (*sognare*)

2. «Alberto, _____ visto il mio libro»? (*avere*)

3. I miei zii _____ molto. (*viaggiare*)

4. Lei _____ il cinema. (*adorare*)

5. «Voi _____ un mucchio di cose»! (*sapere*)

6. Noi _____ il tedesco. (*capire*)

7. Ma loro dove _____? (*andare*)

8. Il gatto? Lui _____ sempre con il mio maglione. (*giocare*)

9. «Tu _____ troppi regali ai bambini». (*fare*)

10. Loro _____ entrare? (*volere*)

Double Subjects

When more than one subject is mentioned, the verb is always in the plural. It is conjugated according to the following pattern:

tu ed io = noi	→	**parliamo**
tu e lui/lei = voi	→	**parlate**
lui e lei = loro	→	**parlano**
lui/lei e loro = loro	→	**parlano**
noi e voi = noi	→	**parliamo**
noi e lui/lei/loro = noi	→	**parliamo**
voi e lui/lei/loro = voi	→	**parlate**

esercizio   1-6

In the following sentences, add the verb in the appropriate person. Use the simple present of the indicative.

1. Noi e voi _____ il film. (*guardare*)

2. Tu e lui _____ sempre a scacchi. (*giocare*)

3. Tu ed io _____ domani. (*partire*)

4. Noi e loro _____ la ditta. (*comprare*)

5. Lui e lei _____ insieme da anni. (*stare*)

6. Voi e loro non _____ abbastanza. (*parlare*)

Addressing People: *Tu/Voi, Lei/Loro*

In Italian there is a familiar, informal address (**dare del tu**) and a polite, formal address (**dare del Lei**):

Forms of address

	INFORMAL		FORMAL	
singular	**tu**	you	**Lei**	you
plural	**voi**	you	**Loro**	you

Tu + *the verb in the second person singular* is used to address a person with whom we are on familiar terms—a family member, friend, or colleague. However, nowadays more and more people use the **tu** form to address strangers as well—in stores, banks, athletic clubs, churches, and so forth.

Tu salti il pranzo oggi?	*Are **you** skipping lunch today?*
Tu sei servita?	*Are **you** being helped?*

Voi + *the verb in the second person plural* is used with a group of people with whom we are on familiar terms and now commonly with a group of strangers as well, especially when giving them instructions or directions. (In writing, you may find **Voi** capitalized, to indicate that it is used to address people directly, but formally.)

Voi prendete il treno o l'aereo?	*Are **you** (pl.) taking the train or the plane?*
Voi dovreste usare l'altra porta, per favore.	***You** (pl.) should use the other door, please.*

Lei + *the verb in the third person singular,* and **Loro** + *the verb in the third person plural* are used to address people formally. (**Loro** is used less and less, except in very formal situations.) **Lei** and **Loro** are often capitalized in writing, and they are also capitalized throughout this book to help readers distinguish them from other uses.

Lei is a feminine pronoun that is used to address both a man and a woman.

Viene anche **Lei** al convegno?	*Are **you** also coming to the conference?*
Mi scusi, **Lei** ha comprato il biglietto?	*Excuse me, did **you** buy the ticket?*

These sentences do not tell us whether the speaker is addressing a man or a woman, but there are times when clues to the gender of the person are present, whereas they may not be in English.

Viene anche **Lei** al convegno, **Dottoressa**?	*Are **you** also coming to the conference, Doctor?*
Lei è il **terzo** a sinistra nella fotografia, Dottor Guidi.	***You** are the third on the right in the photograph, Dr. Guidi.*
Lei è **stata** content**a** del suo acquisto?	*Are **you** pleased with your purchase?*
Lei è **stato** content**o** del suo acquisto?	*Are **you** pleased with your purchase?*

There are many words in Italian that carry gender indicators: adjectives, past participles, nouns indicating titles or other qualifiers, other pronouns, and articles. When possible, *the endings of these words will be masculine* if the person addressed is a man, and *feminine* if the person is a woman.

Nouns indicating professions—**giudice, avvocato, ministro**—do not always take the feminine. You can therefore encounter the following:

È invitat**a** (*fem.*) anche **Lei, Signor giudice** (*masc. noun*)!	***You** are invited too, Madam Judge!*
È invitat**o** anche **Lei, Signor giudice!**	***You** are invited too, Judge! [addressing a man]* or ***You** are invited too, Madam Judge!*

esercizio   1-7

Insert the proper subject, choosing among **lui/Lui, lei/Lei, voi, loro/Loro**. *Quotation marks indicate that the speaker is addressing someone directly.*

1. _____ è una brava ballerina.

2. _____ è andato a Londra.

3. «Signor Rossi, _____ è andato a Londra»?

4. «Signore, _____ ha bisogno di qualcosa»?

5. «Signora, _____ desidera un antipasto»?

6. «_____ partirete con l'autobus delle otto».

7. _____ ha sognato suo padre.

8. «Passi prima _____, Signora Maffei».

9. «Signore e Signori, _____ siano i benvenuti».

10. «_____ avete visto quel film»?

esercizio   1-8

Add the appropriate subject pronouns to the sentences on the right, choosing among **io, tu, lui, lei/Lei, noi, voi, loro/Loro**.

1. io

2. lei

3. noi

4. loro

5. voi

6. Lei

7. tu

8. Loro

9. lui

a. «_____ si spostino, per favore».

b. _____ vanno a sciare.

c. «_____ desidera vedere dei vestiti»?

d. _____ suono il violino.

e. _____ scrivi un articolo.

f. _____ ha vinto alla lotteria. (*Bruno*)

g. _____ telefonate a casa.

h. _____ guida l'aeroplano. (*Giovanna*)

i. _____ salutiamo gli amici.

Esso (*It*) as Subject

Italian does not use **esso** or any other pronoun in cases where English uses *it*:

- To identify a person.

    «Chi è quello là»? «È John».   *"Who is that one over there?" "It's John."*

- With the expressions «**è vero**»? «**non è vero**»? when the antecedents are **nulla** or **tutto** (*nothing, everything/all*).

    Non è successo **niente**, non è vero?   ***Nothing*** *happened,* ***did it?***

- With expressions that refer to time, weather, distances, or the current situation.

    È lunedì.   *It's Monday.*
    È terribile! Sono morti in tantissimi   *It's terrible! So many people died*
      nello tsunami.   *in the tsunami.*

- As a preparatory subject in sentences such as **è necessario, è opportuno, è positivo, è negativo, è probabile, è vero, è falso** (*it's necessary, it's advisable, it's positive, it's negative, it's probable, it's true, it's false*) etc.; **è ora di** (*it's time to . . .*).

    È importante parlargli.   *It's important to talk to him.*
    È ora di andare.   *It's time to go.*

- With impersonal verbs such as **piove, nevica, comincia (a), accade, capita, succede, bisogna, vale la pena** (*it's raining, it's snowing, it begins (to), it happens, it's necessary, it's worthwhile*), etc.

    Piove.   *It's raining.*
    È successo che...   *It happened that . . .*

- As a preparatory subject in sentences such as

    È la mia segretaria che...   *It's my secretary who . . .*
    Sono io che...   *It is I/me who . . .*

esercizio   1-9

Translate the following sentences. Familiarity with interrogative and relative pronouns is necessary to do Exercises 1–10 and 1–11.

1. È meglio andare a casa. _____

2. «Chi bussa alla porta»? «È tua sorella». _____

3. «Che giorno è oggi»? «È giovedì». _____

4. Hai comprato tutto, vero? _____

5. Comincia a nevicare. _____

6. È importante che lui senta la tua versione. _____

7. È il mio medico che ha raccomandato quello specialista. _____

_____

8. Vale la pena parlarle. _____

Placement in Negative Clauses

In negative and interrogative/negative clauses, the subject can be placed *before the negation* and the verb or *after* the verb when we want to add emphasis. (See the following section, "When to Use Subject Pronouns," for rules about their use.)

Io non mangio il pane.	*I don't eat bread.*
Tu non vieni al cinema?	*Aren't you coming to the movies?*
Noi non siamo partiti.	*We didn't leave.*
Non stanno dormendo, loro?	*Aren't they sleeping?*
Lui non può aiutare suo padre.	*He can't help his father.*
Non volete comprare **voi** il libro?	*Don't you want to buy the book?*

esercizio   1-10

Build sentences with the following words and phrases. Conjugate the verb given in italics according to person and number. Use the simple present.

1. tu, il cane, non, *portare* a spasso _____.

2. camminare, non, noi, *andare* a, in montagna, d'inverno _____

_____.

3. *amare*, lei, non, il sushi _____.

4. loro, non, alla zia, *telefonare* _____.

5. *guardare*, voi, il calcio, alla televisione, non _____?

6. dal veterinario, lui, *portare*, non, il gatto _____?

7. *partire*, io, per l'Argentina, non, sabato _____.

8. noi, la casa, non, al mare, *affittare* _____.

When to Use Subject Pronouns

Subject pronouns are used in Italian:

- To emphasize the subject.

    Io ho dato le dimissioni, alla fine.   *I did resign, in the end.*

- To emphasize one subject over another, often inverting the subject + verb word order.

    Io lavoro dalla mattina alla sera,   *I work from morning to night,*
        mentre **tu** ti diverti.   *while **you** are having fun.*
    Ha ragione **lei**, non **lui**.   ***She** is right, not **he**.*

- With verb forms (especially the subjunctive) that could generate confusion about the agent.

    Penso che **tu** non **sia** contento.   *I think that **you** aren't happy.*
    Penso che **lui** non **sia** contento.   *I think that **he** isn't happy.*

esercizio   1-11

Match the subject pronouns on the left with the verb on the right.

1. lei

a. Compro _____ il pane!

2. loro; noi

b. Ha sempre ragione _____ .

3. noi

c. Dovreste stare più attenti, _____ !

4. io

d. Se parlano _____ , non parliamo _____ .

5. voi

e. Se vai _____ , non vado _____ .

6. tu; io

f. Facciamo sempre tutto _____ !

esercizio   1-12

Translate the following sentences.

1. We are not going to Rome, but you (*pl.*) are. _____

2. I use the cellular phone; she doesn't. _____

3. They don't want a dog, but I do. _____

4. He roars; she meows. _____

5. They don't want ice cream; do you (*sing.*)? _____

6. She earns a lot of money; he doesn't. _____

7. He answered; she didn't. _____

8. He barks when he is alone, but she doesn't. _____

Direct Object Pronouns

A direct object is a noun or noun substitute that answers the questions *whom?* or *what?*

*Bob loves **Angela**.*
Question: ***Whom** does John love?*

*John is washing **his car**.*
Question: ***What** is John washing?*

Pronouns that stand for, or replace, a direct object are called *direct object pronouns* (**pronomi complemento oggetto**).

*I called **you**, but you didn't hear **me**.*

*Helen bought new shoes. She wore **them** at Tom's party.*

English has one set of direct object pronouns, which follow the verb. In Italian, direct object pronouns can take two forms: *weak* (**debole**) and *strong* (**forte**).

Weak pronouns are always placed *as close to the verb as possible*. With most modes and tenses, they are placed *before the verb*, but there are some exceptions (see below).

Strong pronouns *need not be placed close to the verb*, but they usually *follow it*.

Pronomi personali complemento oggetto (*Direct object pronouns*)

FORMA DEBOLE (*Weak form*) (*before the verb or attached to it*)	FORMA FORTE (*Strong form*)	Direct object pronoun (*usually after the verb*)
mi	**me**	me
ti	**te**	you
lo	**lui**	him
lo/la/La	**lei/Lei**	her
lo/la	—	it
ci	**noi**	us
vi	**voi**	you
li/le/Li/Le	**loro/Loro**	them (*people, pets*)
li/le	—	them (*things*)

Mi pagano.	*They pay **me**.*
Pagano **me**.	*They pay **me**.*
Ci contattano.	*They contact **us**.*
Contattano **noi**.	*They contact **us**.*
La nutro.	*I feed **her** (my cat).*
Nutro **lei**.	*I feed **her** (my cat).*

In the third person singular and plural, *strong forms* are not used for things or for animals that are not household pets.

Mia zia ha comprato le scarpe.	→	Mia zia **le** ha comprate.	[*Not*: Mia zia ha comprato **loro**.]
My aunt bought the shoes.	→	*My aunt bought **them**.*	
Hanno catturato le iene.	→	**Le** hanno catturate.	[*Not*: Hanno catturato **loro**.]
They captured the hyenas.	→	*They captured **them**.*	

In colloquial Italian, *strong forms* are used when we want to *emphasize the direct object, or to contrast two objects*.

Voglio **lui** come testimone!	*I want **him** as my best man!*
Ha aiutato **voi**, ma non ha aiutato **noi**.	*She helped **you** but didn't help **us**.*

esercizio   2-1

*Replace the words in parentheses with the appropriate weak forms of the direct object pronouns, choosing among **mi**, **ti**, **lo/la**, **ci**, **vi**, **li**, **le**. Place them before the verb.*

1. _____ cercano. (il dottore)

2. _____ guardate? (il film)

3. Giovanni _____ porta al mare. (i figli)

4. _____ batto sempre a scacchi. (Angela)

5. _____ chiami? (il cane)

6. _____ raccolgono. (le rose)

7. _____ mangi? (la torta)

8. _____ nutre. (i piccoli)

9. _____ porti in casa? (le sedie)

10. _____ aiutano. (le loro amiche)

esercizio   2-2

Replace the words in parentheses with the strong forms of the direct object pronouns, choosing among **me, te, lui, lei, noi, voi, loro**. *Place them after the verb.* **Lui, lei, loro** *are used for pets but not for things. Leave the sentence blank if you cannot use a strong pronoun.*

1. Cercano _____. (*il dottore*)

2. Guardate _____? (*il film*)

3. Giovanni porta _____ al mare. (*i figli*)

4. Batto sempre _____ a scacchi. (*Angela*)

5. Chiami _____? (*il cane*)

6. Raccolgono _____. (*le rose*)

7. Mangi _____? (*la torta*)

8. Nutre _____. (*i piccoli*)

9. Porti _____ in casa? (*le sedie*)

10. Aiutano _____. (*le loro amiche*)

Formal and Informal Address

Italian uses direct object pronouns in addressing people, either formally or informally; **vi/voi** are also used to address a group of people formally.

Forms of address

	FAMILIAR		POLITE			
	weak	*strong*	*weak*	*strong*		
singular	**ti**	**te**	**La**	**Lei**	you	
plural	**vi**	**voi**	**Li/Le**	**Loro**	you	

Weak forms are placed *before the verb.*

Ti invito a cena, Joe.   *I'm inviting **you** to dinner, Joe.*
Vi invito a cena, Lia e John.   *I'm inviting **you** to dinner, Lia and Joe.*
La invito a cena, Signor**e**.   *I'm inviting **you** to dinner, Sir.*
Vi/Li invito a cena, Signor**i**.   *I'm inviting **you** to dinner, gentlemen.*
La invito a cena, Signor**a**.   *I'm inviting **you** to dinner, Madam.*
Vi/Le invito a cena, Signor**e**.   *I'm inviting **you** to dinner, ladies.*

Strong forms *follow the verb.*

Invito **te** a cena, Joe.   *I invite **you** to dinner, Joe.*
Invito **Lei** a cena, Signora.   *I invite **you** to dinner, Madam.*

esercizio   2-3

*Translate the following sentences. Use the appropriate pronoun, choosing among **ti**, **La**, **vi**. Use **vi** for both formal and informal situations when addressing more than one person. Last names indicate that people are on formal terms. Use the simple present to translate both the present progressive and the future.*

1. Is he (*sing.*) calling you? _____

2. I will contact you soon, Mr. Vanzetti. _____

3. I know you well, guys (*ragazzi*). _____

4. We are inviting you (*pl.*) to dinner. _____

5. I call you (*sing.*) every day. _____

6. I'll see you at the bar, madam. _____

7. We'll take you to the airport, gentlemen. _____

esercizio   2-4

*In the following conversation, insert **mi** or **ti**, placing them before the verb.*

Pietro: «_____ chiamavi»?
Giulia: «Sì, _____ chiamavo. Ho bisogno di un favore. _____ porti in montagna»?
Pietro: «Non _____ porto in montagna, perché devo andare a Milano. Quando torno, vuoi andare a cena da mia sorella»?
Giulia: «Preferirei di no. Quando _____ trovo in casa da solo»?
Pietro: «_____ trovi domani sera. Vieni, così facciamo due chiacchiere in pace».

esercizio   2-5

*In the following conversation insert **te** or **me**, placing them after the verb.*

Pietro: «Chiamavi _____ o lui»?
Giulia: «Chiamavo _____. Ho bisogno di un favore. Domani, porti _____ ed i miei amici in montagna»?
Pietro: «Non porto _____ ed i tuoi amici in montagna, perché devo andare a Milano. Quando torno, vuoi andare a cena da mia sorella»?
Giulia: «Preferirei di no. Quando trovo _____ da solo»?
Pietro: «Trovi _____ da solo domani sera. Vieni, così facciamo due chiacchiere in pace».

Placement in Negative Clauses

In negative clauses, the negative particle **non** is placed directly before the verb. The weak forms of the direct object pronouns are placed *between the negation and the verb*; the strong forms follow the verb.

Lo vedo.	Vedo **lui**.	*I see **him**.*
Non lo vedo.	**Non** vedo **lui**.	*I don't see **him**.*
Non lo vedi?	**Non** vedi **lui**?	***Don't** you see **him**?*

esercizio   2-6

*Answer the following questions in both the affirmative and in the negative, using the weak pronouns **mi, ti, lo/la, ci, vi, li/le**, which are placed before the verb.*

1. Compri il vino? _____   _____

2. Avvisa i suoi genitori? _____   _____

3. Pulisci la tua stanza? _____   _____

4. Guardate le Olimpiadi? _____   _____

5. Giulia ama molto l'opera?   _____   _____

6. Rileggono la senatrice?   _____   _____

7. Approva il primo ministro?   _____   _____

8. Invitate i vostri amici a pranzo?   _____   _____

9. Portiamo tua zia al mare?   _____   _____

esercizio   2-7

*Answer the same sentences in both the affirmative and the negative, using the strong pronouns **me, te, lui, lei, noi,
voi, loro**, which follow the verb. Remember that **lui, lei,** and **loro** are not used for things or for animals (except for
pets). Leave the sentence blank if you cannot use a weak pronoun.*

1. Compri il vino?   _____   _____

2. Avvisa i suoi genitori?   _____   _____

3. Pulisci la tua stanza?   _____   _____

4. Guardate le Olimpiadi?   _____   _____

5. Giulia ama molto l'opera?   _____   _____

6. Rileggono la senatrice?   _____   _____

7. Approva il primo ministro?   _____   _____

8. Invitate i vostri amici a pranzo?   _____   _____

9. Portiamo tua zia al mare?   _____   _____

Placement with the Infinitive

With the infinitive, the *weak forms* of the direct object pronouns are *attached to the verb,* dropping
the last vowel:

vedere	→	*vederti,* -ci, ecc.
chiamare	→	**chiamarlo, -li**, ecc.
Chiamar**mi**.		*To call **me**.*
Pagar**la**.		*To pay **her**.*

Strong forms follow the infinitive.

Chiamare **me**.	*To call **me**.*
Pagare **lei**.	*To pay **her**.*

esercizio	2-8

Replace the strong pronouns with weak pronouns, attaching them to the infinitive.

1. Pensi di aiutare lui? _____

2. Ha deciso di assumere lei? _____

3. Sei sicura di battere lui a dama? _____

4. Vi siete ricordati di salutare loro? _____

5. Credono di aiutare noi. _____

6. Ho i soldi per pagare voi. _____

7. Vengono a trovare me. _____

8. È contento di vedere te. _____

Placement with the Imperative

With the positive form of the imperative (in the second person singular and plural only), *the weak forms* of the direct object pronouns *are attached directly to the verb.*

Chiama**li**!	*Call **them**!*
Pagate**ci**!	*Pay **us**!*

With the *negative form of the imperative*, the *weak* forms of the direct object pronouns can be placed *after the verb*, or *between the negation and the verb*. In the second person singular, because the verb is in the infinitive, the last vowel of the verb will be dropped when we attach the pronoun directly to it.

Non chiamar**li**!	Non **li** chiamare!	*Don't call **them**!*
Non chiamate**li**!	Non **li** chiamate!	*Don't call **them**!*

Strong forms follow the verb.

Chiama **lui**!	*Call **him**!*
Chiama **loro**!	*Call **them**!*
Non chiamare **lui**!	*Don't call **him**!*
Non chiamare **loro**!	*Don't call **them**!*

esercizio   2-9

Replace the nouns/names with direct object pronouns. Use the weak forms, attaching them directly to the verb.

1. Porta le sedie in casa! _____

2. Non mangiare tutto il gelato! _____

3. Aiutate vostra sorella! _____

4. Non comprate la frutta. _____

5. Porta il libro, mi raccomando. _____

6. Saluta Elisa da parte mia! _____

7. Non seguite Mario! _____

8. Invita Marco e Gianna a cena! _____

Direct Object Pronouns with Compound Tenses (*Tempi Composti*)

Tenses may be *simple* (**semplici**) (*I see, I think, I heard*, etc.) or *compound* (**composti**) (*I'm listening, I have seen*, etc.).

Weak forms of the direct object pronouns are placed *before* the verb form, not between its components.

Li ho chiamat**i**.	*I called **them**.*
Non **li** ho chiamat**i**.	*I didn't call **them**.*

We can also attach the weak forms to the gerund, which is used to convey the *present progressive*.

Lo sto chiamando.	Sto chiamando**lo**.	*I'm calling **him**.*
Non **lo** sto chiamando.	Non sto chiamando**lo**.	*I'm not calling **him**.*

The present progressive is formed with the verb **stare**, which behaves like the auxiliary **avere** when it accompanies a verb followed by a direct object. Strong forms follow the verb.

Ho chiamato **loro**.	*I called **them**.*
Sto chiamando **loro**.	*I'm calling **them**.*

esercizio | **2-10**

Replace the strong forms of the direct object pronouns with the corresponding weak forms attached to the verb.

1. Giovanna sta avvertendo lui. _____

2. Stiamo chiamando voi. _____

3. Stanno pagando noi. _____

4. Mia sorella sta ringraziando te. _____

5. State aiutando loro? _____

6. I miei amici stanno seguendo lei. _____

7. Sta osservando me. _____

Coordination of Direct Object Pronouns with the Past Participle

Italian uses the present perfect (**hai mangiato**, **ho letto**, ecc.) in many cases where English uses the simple perfect (*I went, I read,* etc.).

Ho visitato Atene tre anni fa. *I **visited** Athens three years ago.*

When the verb carries a direct object, the past participle of the verb (**comprato, chiamato, aiutato**) is coordinated with *the gender and number of the direct object* when the object *precedes* the verb, but not when it follows it.

L(o)'ho sentit**o**. Ho vist**o lui**. *I saw **him**.*
L(a)'ho sentit**a**. Ho vist**o lei**. *I saw **her**.*

The masculine is used when the gender of the person is not known, or when the object includes both males and females.

Li ho vist**i**. Ho vist**o loro**. *I saw **them** (masc. pl.).*
Le ho vist**e**. Ho vist**o loro**. *I saw **them** (fem. pl.).*

esercizio | **2-11**

*Answer the following questions in the affirmative and in the negative, using the weak pronouns **mi, ti, lo/la, ci, vi, li/le**, which are placed before the verb. Take your clues to the gender of the object from the nouns in the interrogative sentences.*

1. Hai comprato il vino? _____ _____

2. Ha avvisato i suoi genitori? _____ _____

3. Hai pulito la tua stanza?   _____   _____

4. Avete guardato le Olimpiadi?   _____   _____

5. Maria ha visto sua cugina?   _____   _____

6. Hanno rieletto la senatrice?   _____   _____

7. Avete invitato i vostri amici a pranzo? _____   _____

8. Hanno portato tua zia al mare?   _____   _____

Placement with Modal Auxiliaries (*Verbi Servili*)

When used as modifiers of another verb, the modal auxiliaries **dovere** (*must*), **potere** (*may/can*), **volere** (*will*), and **sapere** (*to know*) are followed by the infinitive.

Devo partire.	*I must leave.*
So ballare.	*I can dance.*

In affirmative and negative clauses, weak forms can be either placed before the modal verb or attached to the verb in the infinitive.

Posso aiutar**la**.	**La** posso aiutare.	*I can help **her**.*
Devo guardar**lo**.	**Lo** devo guardare.	*I must watch **him**.*
Non posso veder**lo**.	Non **lo** posso vedere.	*I can't see **him**.*

There is no set rule about where to place the weak forms; it is a matter of emphasis, meaning, and style, but *the version with the pronoun attached to the infinitive is more common.*

Strong forms follow the verb in the infinitive.

Posso aiutare **lei**.	*I can help **her**.*
Devo guardare **lui**.	*I must watch **him**.*
Non posso vedere **lui**.	*I can't see **him**.*

esercizio   2-12

*Replace the nouns or the names with direct object pronouns, choosing among **mi, ti, lo/la, ci, vi, loro**, placing them either before the modal auxiliary or after the verb in the infinitive.*

1. Possiamo servire gli ospiti?   _____   _____

2. Vuoi aiutare mia sorella?   _____   _____

3. Devono invitare il loro capo.   _____   _____

4. Vogliamo pagare il consulente? _____   _____

5. Sa scrivere la lettera. _____   _____

6. Devo guardare la pietanza. _____   _____

7. Potete aprire la porta. _____   _____

8. Sanno riparare il computer? _____   _____

esercizio   2-13

Translate the following sentences. Use both weak and strong pronouns, depending on the emphasis you want to give the sentence. Remember that Italian uses the present perfect more than English does.

1. You wanted a new dress. Were you able to buy it?

   _____

2. You shouldn't have paid them. They didn't finish their job.

   _____

3. You're asking me if I want to invite him, too? Absolutely not!

   _____

4. The organizers assigned our tennis partners. I definitely did not want her.

   _____

5. We caught a lot of crabs. Can they eat them?

   _____

6. She loves her sister very much. She wants to help her as much as she can.

   _____

7. They must convince them to come.

   _____

Note: In a compound tense, we cannot attach a pronoun directly to the past participle (**aver amato, aver guardato, aver visto, aver preso,** ecc.). When the compound tense is made of a modal verb, an infinitive, and a past participle, the weak form of the direct object pronoun can be attached to the infinitive followed by the past participle:

Devono aver**li** convinti a venire. /   *They must have convinced **them** to come.*
    Li devono avere convinti a venire.

The strong forms follow the verb.

Devono aver convinto **loro** a venire.   *They must have convinced **them** to come.*

Other Modal Auxiliaries

Other verbs can play a modal function: **desiderare, osare, preferire, sembrare**. When followed by a verb in the infinitive that carries a direct object, the general rule is to use the pronouns **mi, lo, ci, li**, ecc., attached to the verb in the infinitive.

Desidero veder**lo**.   *I wish to see **him**.*
Preferiscono chiamar**vi** domani.   *They prefer to call **you** tomorrow.*

Lasciare and *Fare* + the Infinitive

The causative verbs **lasciare** (*to let*) and **fare** (*to have something done by someone else; to make someone else do something*) allow or cause a person other than the subject to perform the action.

The weak forms of the direct object pronouns *must be placed before* **lasciare** or **fare**.

Lo lascio andare. [*Not:* Lascio andar**lo**.]   *I let **him** go.*
L(a)'ho fatta andare dal dottore.   *I had/made **her** go to the doctor.*
    [*Not:* Ho fatto andar**la** dal dottore.]

Strong forms are placed after the infinitive.

Lascio andare **lui, non lei**.   *I let **him** go, not **her**.*
Ha fatto andare **me** a chiedere scusa. *She had/made **me** go and apologize.*

esercizio   2-14

*Translate the following sentences using the modal auxiliaries or the verbs **lasciare/fare** suggested in parentheses, followed by an infinitive. Use the weak forms of the direct object pronouns.*

1. Pietro dared reproach her. (*osare*) _____

2. Clara seems to understand me. (*sembrare*) _____

3. We let them leave. (*lasciare*) _____

4. You (*pl.*) make me eat too many candies. (*fare*) _____

5. They prefer to contact you (*sing.*) directly. (*preferire*) _____

6. I'll let (*pres. simple*) you (*sing.*) buy that dress. (*lasciare*) _____

7. You (*sing.*) made her cry. (*fare*) _____

8. He let me cry. (*lasciare*) _____

Lo (It/That)

The weak pronoun **lo** can refer to the entire sentence preceding it. English can use *it/that* with the same function, but often omits it.

Ho parlato con Luigi; tutti **lo** hanno **notato**.	*I spoke with Luigi; everyone **noticed** (it).*
«Ho visto Nicoletta ieri». «**Lo so**».	*"I saw Nicoletta yesterday." "**I know**."*
Si crede bella, ma **non lo è**.	*She thinks she's beautiful, but **she isn't**.*

esercizio	2-15

*In the following sentences, insert the pronoun **lo** in the proper place. Its placement follows the same rules as those of any other weak direct object pronoun.*

1. «Vorrei tanto aiutarti, ma non ho un soldo». «Capisco». _____

2. «La nostra squadra vincerà sicuramente». «Chi dice»? _____

3. Si crede intelligente, ma non è. _____

4. Vuole tornare; non ha detto, ma ho capito. _____

5. Ha giocato solo con Lucia. Hai notato? _____

6. Volevi andare in montagna. Hai poi fatto? _____

7. «Hanno divorziato». «Ho saputo». _____

Ci (Vi): Other Uses

Besides functioning as direct object pronouns, *ci* (and *vi,* rarely used) can be used to mean:

here, there, in that place, through there

C'è... /**Ci sono...** (**Vi è...** /**Vi sono...**) translate as *There is . . . /There are . . .*

Ci sono tanti fiori nel prato.	*There are so many flowers in the meadow.*
C'è molto da fare.	*There is a lot to do.*

C'era una volta un re crudele...   *Once upon a time there was*
  [*Not*: **V'era una volta...**]   *a cruel king . . .*
Ci vado spesso.   *I go **there** often.*
Ci passo tutti i giorni.   *I go **through there** every day.*
Ci sei, se passo stasera?   ***Will you be in**, if I stop by tonight?*

This/That

Non **ci** fare caso.   →   Non fare caso **a ciò/a quello**.   *Don't mind **that**.*
Non **ci** capisco nulla.   →   Non capisco nulla **di ciò**.   *I don't get any **of that**.*

---

esercizio   2-16

---

*Translate the following sentences. As a direct object pronoun, use **ci** placed before the verb in a finite form or attached to the infinitive.*

1. There are too many books on the shelf. _____

2. They can see us from the street. _____

3. I'll go there (*simple pres.*) tomorrow. _____

4. Once upon a time there was a gentle dragon . . . _____

   _____

5. Are you (*pl.*) in, if I stop (*passare*) by tonight? _____

6. She thought (*ha pensato*) a lot about it, but she refused (*ha rifiutato*). _____

   _____

7. There is a lot of bread at home. _____

Indirect Object Pronouns

An indirect object is a noun or noun substitute that usually requires a preposition to make the sentence meaningful: "I'm going with Sandra" becomes meaningless if we say "I'm going Sandra." Pronouns that stand for or replace an indirect object are called *indirect object pronouns* (**pronomi complemento indiretto**).

> *I'm going **with Sandra**.* → *I'm going **with her**.*

One of the most frequently used indirect objects is the one that answers the questions: **To/for whom** is something being done?

> *She wrote **to Peter**.*   *We bought a cake **for Mary**.*
> Question: ***To whom***   Question: ***For whom*** *did we*
> *did she write?*   *buy a cake?*

Pronouns can replace names or nouns as indirect objects *to/for whom/which* the action is aimed.

> *She wrote a letter **to him**.*   *We bought a cake **for her**.*

This construction is used so often in everyday language that the prepositions *to* and *for* can be omitted.

> *She wrote **him** a letter.*   *We bought **her** a cake.*

What we just said about English holds also for Italian, which can use:

- The *strong* forms of the object pronouns (see Unit 2), accompanied by the prepositions **a/per**.

> Ha parlato **a lui**.   *He talked **to him**.*
> Compri un vestito   *Are you buying a dress*
> **per lei**?   *for her?*

- The *weak* object pronoun, used without a preposition.

> **Gli** hai parlato?   *Did you talk **to him**?*
> **Le** compri un vestito?   *Are you buying **her** a dress?*

The following table lists personal pronouns conveying end or purpose.

Pronomi personali complemento indiretto (*Indirect object pronouns*)

FORMA DEBOLE (*Weak form*)	FORMA FORTE (*Strong form*)	INDIRECT OBJECT Pronouns
mi	**a/per me**	to/for me
ti	**a/per te**	to/for you
gli	**a/per lui**	to/for him
le/Le	**a/per lei/Lei**	to/for her
ci	**a/per noi**	to/for us
vi	**a/per voi**	to/for you
(gli)	**loro/Loro** and **a/per loro**	to/for them

There is no weak form for the third person plural. The *masculine singular* **gli** is now currently used for the masculine and feminine plural.

Parlo **a Carlo.**	→	**Gli** parlo.	*I'm talking to him.*
Parlo **ad Anna.**	→	**Le** parlo.	*I'm talking to her.*
Parlo **ad Anna e Carlo.**	→	**Gli** parlo.	*I'm talking to them.*

The strong pronoun **loro/Loro** is used for both masculine and feminine.

Parlo **ad Anna e Carlo.**	→	Parlo **loro.** / Parlo **a loro.**	*I'm talking to them.*

Placement of Strong Forms in Affirmative and Negative Clauses: *a me (to Me)/a voi (to You)*, etc.

Per me, a lui, a voi, ecc., are used when we want to clarify or emphasize the person to whom the action is addressed.

Strong forms are usually placed *after the verb*. They are never placed between the negative particle **non** and the verb.

Hanno scritto **a noi.**	*They wrote to us.*
Non hanno scritto **a noi.**	*They didn't write to us.*
[*Not*: **Non a noi** hanno scritto.]	

When the sentence includes a *direct object*, strong pronouns can be placed *before or after the direct object*.

Offriamo **a voi un viaggio gratuito.**	*We offer a free trip to you.*
Ho comprato **una giacca nuova per te.**	*I bought a new jacket for you.*

When **loro** is used without a preposition, *it must be placed directly after the verb.*

Comunicai **loro** la notizia.	*I gave them the news.*
Ho spiegato il problema **a loro.**	*I explained the problem to them.*

esercizio	3-1

Rewrite the following sentences, using a pronoun preceded by a preposition to express the indirect object.

1. She writes him long letters. _____

2. We offered you a ride. _____

3. I sent you a package. _____

4. They bought her a car. _____

5. He gave them a suggestion. _____

6. You sold them her jewelry. _____

7. Do me a favor. _____

esercizio	3-2

*Translate the following sentences using the strong pronouns with a preposition, following the same word order as in the English sentences. Use **a loro** for the third person plural. Use the simple present.*

1. We are buying a present for you (*pl*). _____

2. Are you (*sing.*) writing to her? _____

3. Are they offering help to us? _____

4. Is she talking to you (*sing.*)? _____

5. I'm giving him a piece of advice. _____

6. Are you (*pl.*) calling (*telefonare*) them? _____

7. He is sending a package to me. _____

esercizio	3-3

*Translate the following sentences using the strong pronouns with a preposition. Place them directly after the verb. Use **loro** without a preposition for the third person plural. Use the verb suggested in parentheses.*

1. We said good-bye to them. (*dire arrivederci*) _____

2. She entrusted her investments to him. (*affidare*) _____

3. He told me the end of the movie! (*raccontare*) _____

4. You two promised her not to lie anymore! (*dire le bugie*) _____

_____

5. He told them his version of the incident. _____

Placement of Weak Forms in Affirmative and Negative Clauses: *mi* (*to Me*), *ti* (*to You*), *gli* (*to Him*), etc.

In affirmative clauses, weak pronouns are placed *before* the verb form, with both simple and compound tenses. In negative clauses they are placed *between the negative particle* **non** and *the verb*. The verb may or may not be followed by a direct object.

Gli parlo.	*I will speak **to him**.*
Non gli parlo. [*Not:* **Gli non** parlo.]	*I'm not talking **to him**.*
Le ho detto **una bugia**.	*I told **her a lie**.*
Non le ho detto una bugia.	*I didn't tell **her** a lie.*
[*Not:* **Le non** ho detto una bugia.]	
Le stai offrendo **un lavoro**?	*Are you offering **her a job**?*
Non mi stai offrendo un lavoro?	*Aren't you offering **me** a job?*
[*Not:* **Mi non** stai offrendo un lavoro?]	

esercizio   3-4

Replace the subject pronouns in parentheses with the appropriate indirect object pronouns. Choose among **mi, ti, le, gli, ci, vi, gli,** *which are placed before the verb. Use* **gli** *for the third person plural.*

1. _____ compriamo un gelato. (*voi*)

2. _____ raccontano una storia. (*egli*)

3. _____ mando dei fiori. (*lei*)

4. _____ offre il suo aiuto. (*noi*)

5. _____ compro un televisore. (*loro*)

6. _____ scrivi una cartolina? (*io*)

7. _____ regalo il mio orologio. (*tu*)

esercizio	3-5

*Translate the following sentences. Remember that you can use **gli** for the singular and the plural. Use the verb suggested in parentheses.*

1. Does she care for him? (*voler bene*) _____

2. I tell them everything. (*dire*) _____

3. Why don't you tell them your story? (*raccontare*) _____

4. We'll give (*simple pres.*) them a new TV set. (*regalare*) _____

5. I promise you (*pl.*) better service next time. (*promettere*) _____

6. Her lover buys her very expensive jewelry. (*comprare*) _____

esercizio	3-6

Translate the following sentences using the weak pronouns, which go before the verb. Use the verb suggested in parentheses.

1. We said good-bye to them. (*dire arrivederci*) _____

2. She entrusted her investments to him. (*affidare*) _____

3. He told me the end of the movie! (*raccontare*) _____

4. You two promised her not to lie anymore! (*promettere*) _____

5. He told them his version of the incident. (*dire*) _____

Placement with the Infinitive

With the verb in the infinitive, the *weak forms* of the indirect object pronouns are attached to the verb, dropping the last vowel.

Parlar**mi**.   *To talk **to me**.*
Ha deciso di dar**ci** un passaggio.   *He decided to give **us** a ride.*

Strong forms follow the verb. **Loro** can follow the verb without any preposition.

Parlare **a noi**.   *To speak **to us**.*
Ho deciso di dare **loro** un passaggio.   *I decided to give **them** a ride.*

Replace the strong pronouns with indirect object pronouns, attached to the verb in the infinitive.

1. Pensi di telefonare a lui? _____

2. Ha deciso di offrire a lei il lavoro? _____

3. Hai tempo di spiegare a noi quel problema? _____

4. Hanno deciso di dare a voi le informazioni. _____

5. Pensano di parlare a te delle vacanze. _____

6. Sai scrivere un bel biglietto di auguri *per lei?* _____

7. Crede di fare un favore *a me?* _____

Placement with the Imperative, Second Person Singular and Plural

With the positive form of the imperative, the *weak forms* of the indirect object pronouns are attached to the verb.

Parla**mi**!	*Talk **to me**!*
Parlate**mi**!	*Don't talk **to me**!*

With the verb in the negative, the weak pronouns can be *attached to the infinitive* or be placed *between the negation and the verb.*

Non parlar**mi**!	**Non mi** parlare!	*Don't talk **to me**!*
Non parlate**mi**!	Non **mi** parlate!	*Don't talk **to me**!*

Strong forms follow the verb. **Loro** follows the verb, with or without a preposition.

Parla **a lui**!	*Talk **to him**.*
Non parlare **a lui**!	***Don't** talk **to him**!*
Parla **a loro** di tuo fratello!	*Talk **to them** about your brother!*
Non parlare **loro** di tuo fratello!	***Don't** talk **to them** about your brother!*

Replace the strong pronouns with the weak forms of the indirect object pronouns attached directly to the verb.

1. Parla a lui del problema con i vicini! _____

2. Non dire a me che sei stanca! _____

3. Raccontate a noi i vostri progetti! _____

4. Non consegnate a lei il pacco! _____

5. Non offrire a lei la cena! _____

Indirect Object Pronouns with Compound Tenses

With compound tenses (e.g., the present progressive *I am listening, I have heard,* etc.), the weak forms of the indirect object pronouns are placed *before or after* the verb form, not between its components.

Gli ho detto la verità.	*I told **him** the truth.*
Non gli ho detto la verità.	*I **didn't** tell **him** the truth.*

With the present progressive, which uses the gerund, *weak pronouns* can be placed either *before* the verb form or *attached* to the gerund.

Gli sto parlando.
Sto parlando**gli**.   } *I'm talking **to him**.*

Strong forms follow the verb form.

Ho detto la verità **a lui**.	*I'm telling **him** the truth.*
Sto parlando **a lui**.	*I'm talking **to him**.*

esercizio   3-9

Replace the strong forms of the indirect object pronouns with the corresponding weak forms. Attach them to the verb when possible.

1. Ho scritto una lettera a lei. _____

2. Sta telefonando a lui. _____

3. Abbiamo fatto un regalo a voi. _____

4. Hanno offerto un passaggio a noi. _____

5. Stai mandando un e-mail a me? _____

6. Sto comprando un libro per te. _____

Placement with Modal Auxiliaries (*Verbi Servili*)

With the modal auxiliaries **dovere** (*must*), **potere** (*may/can*), **volere** (*will*), **sapere** (*to know*), followed by an infinitive, the indirect object pronouns **mi, ti, gli,** ecc., (weak forms) can be placed *before* the modal auxiliary, or *after* the verb in the infinitive, in both affirmative and negative clauses. There is no set rule about where to place the indirect weak pronouns.

Posso mandar**vi** una lettera.	**Vi** posso mandare una lettera.	*I can send* **you** *a letter.*
Non posso mandar**vi** una lettera.	**Non vi** posso mandare una lettera.	*I can't send* **you** *a letter.*

Strong forms follow the last infinitive, either before or after the direct object, if one is present.

Posso mandare **a voi** una lettera.	*I can send* **you** *a letter.*
Posso mandare una lettera **a voi**.	*I can send a letter* **to you**.

When addressing a person formally, **Le** is used for either a man or a woman.

«Posso offrir**Le** un aperitivo»?

may mean

"May I offer you an aperitif, Madam?"

or

"May I offer you an aperitif, Sir?"

esercizio   3-10

Replace the strong forms of the indirect object pronouns in parentheses with the corresponding weak forms, **mi, ti, le,** *ecc. Place them after the infinitive. Use* **vi** *to address a group of people formally or informally.*

1. Posso parlare (*a Lei*), Signora? _____

2. Posso presentare (*a Lei*) mia moglie, Signore? _____

3. Vorrei offrire (*a te*) una cena. _____

4. Vogliono parlare (*a noi*) di un progetto. _____

5. Dovete consegnare (*a me*) un pacco? _____

6. Possiamo offrire (*a voi*) qualcosa da bere, Signori? _____

7. Devi confessare (*a lui*) il tuo errore. _____

Other Modal Auxiliaries

When the verbs **desiderare**, **osare**, **preferire**, **sembrare**, ecc., are followed by another verb in the infinitive that carries an indirect object pronoun, the pronouns **mi, gli, le, ci**, ecc., *are attached to the verb in the infinitive.*

Desidero scriver**le**.	*I wish to write **to her**.*
Preferiscono parlar**vi**.	*They prefer to talk **to you**.*

Strong forms follow the infinitive.

Desidero scrivere **a lei**.	*I wish to write **to her**.*
Preferiscono parlare **a voi**.	*They prefer to talk **to you**.*

esercizio | **3-11**

*Translate the following sentences using the causative or modal auxiliary suggested in parentheses. Use the **mi, gli, le, ci**, ecc., indirect pronouns.*

1. Do you (*pl.*) wish to give her a suggestion? _____

2. She lets me eat her slice of cake. _____

3. They dared talk to him. _____

4. She had a gift sent to us. (*fare*) _____

5. We didn't let him finish his speech. _____

6. He seems to believe him. (*sembrare*) _____

7. Do you (*sing.*) prefer to buy her a CD? (*preferire*) _____

8. She doesn't let them use her car. _____

Causative Verbs (Verbi Causativi): Lasciare, Fare

The causative verbs **lasciare** (*to let*) and **fare** (*to have something done by someone else; to make someone else do something*) can be followed by a verb that carries both a direct object and an indirect object pronoun. The weak forms **mi, gli, vi**, ecc., *must* be placed *before* the causative verb.

Gli lascio finire la vacanza.	*I'll let **him** finish his vacation.*
[*Not:* Lascio finir**gli** la vacanza.]	
Vi faccio mandare un messaggio.	*I'll have a message sent **to you**.*
[*Not:* Faccio mandar**vi** un messaggio.]	
Ci lasciano usare la loro barca.	*They let **us** use their boat.*
[*Not:* Lasciano usar**ci** la loro barca.]	
Le fate finire il lavoro?	*Will you have **her** finish that job?*
[*Not:* Fate finir**le** il lavoro.]	

Strong forms follow the infinitive.

Lascio finire la vacanza **a lui**.   *I let **him** finish his vacation.*

Indirect Object Pronouns with *Piacere (to Please)*

The Italian verb **piacere** (*to please*) is used to convey the idea that English conveys with the verb *to like*. In English, we say: "Mary likes the dog."

In Italian, the *object* of the verb (the dog) becomes the *subject*. The *subject* of the sentence (I) becomes the person *to whom the dog is pleasing*. And since in Italian the subject of the sentence is the person or thing that is pleasing, *the verb agrees with the subject*, not with the recipient of the action.

A Maria **piace il cane**. /   *Maria likes the dog.*
  Il cane piace a Maria.   (Literally: ***The dog is pleasing** to Maria.*)
A mio fratello **piacciono i video games**.   *My brother likes video games.*
          (Literally: ***Video games are pleasing** to my brother.*)

Instead of a noun or a name preceded by the preposition **a**, we can use an *indirect object pronoun*. The *weak forms* of the indirect object pronouns are placed *before* the verb.

Le piace la torta.   ***She** likes the cake.*
Gli piacciono i nuovi sci.   ***He** likes the new skis.*

Strong forms can be placed either before or after the verb, but preferably *before*. This construction is commonly used, since it helps emphasize what the person likes or does not like.

Rego prep
A me piacciono i dolci.   *I like sweets.*
Il salmone piace **a lei**.   ***She** likes salmon.*

In negative clauses, *weak pronouns* are placed *between the negative particle* **non** *and the verb*. *Strong pronouns* are placed *before the negation or after the verb*.

Non le piace la carne.   *She **doesn't** like meat.*
A voi non piace il vino. /   *You **don't** like wine.*
  Il vino **non piace a voi**.

In Italian there are several verbs that work in the same way as **piacere**. The most common are:

accadere/capitare/succedere	to happen to someone
bastare	to be sufficient to/to be enough for someone; to suffice to someone
dispiacere	to be displeased with; to be sorry about (used for feelings and mental states rather than things)
far bene	to be good for someone; to be beneficial to someone

far male	to hurt (someone); to ache
far piacere	to please someone; to be pleasing to someone
far dispiacere	to displease someone
importare (di)	to matter to someone
interessare	to be interested in; to interest someone
mancare	to lack; to miss
parere/sembrare	to seem/appear to someone

esercizio   3-12

Change the following sentences from "I like (someone/something)" to "(Someone/ something) is pleasing to me."

1. We like ice cream. _____

2. She likes books. _____

3. You (*pl.*) like that dog. _____

4. They don't like cats. _____

5. You (*sing.*) like Anna. _____

6. He likes movies. _____

7. I like the tango. _____

esercizio   3-13

Translate the following sentences using the verb **piacere**. *Use the weak forms of the indirect object pronouns, placed before the verb. Use* **gli** *for the third person singular and plural.*

1. Do you like the cinema? _____

2. He doesn't like meat. _____

3. We don't like the prime minister. _____

4. I don't like those books. _____

5. They don't like the new house. _____

6. She likes your brothers. _____

7. I like jazz. _____

8. You (*sing.*) don't like jazz. _____

esercizio	3-14

*Translate the following sentences. Use the strong forms of the indirect object pronouns with the preposition **a**. Place them before the verb.*

1. Did they like the opera? _____

2. You (*pl.*) didn't like that restaurant. _____

3. He didn't like the soup. _____

4. She liked her trip. _____

5. Did you (*sing.*) like their CDs? _____

6. She likes your brothers. _____

7. I like jazz, you (*sing.*) don't. _____

8. We liked the movie, you (*pl.*) didn't. _____

Double Pronouns

A sentence can contain *both a direct object and an indirect object*, which can be expressed through either names/nouns or pronouns.

> *You gave **a present** (**it**)*   →   *You gave **it** to her.*
> *to Christina (**to her**).*

Italian can:

- Place the *direct object pronoun before the verb* and *the indirect object* accompanied by the prepositions **a**/**per** *after the verb*.

   Lo hai portato **a me**.   *You brought **it** to me.*
   Le ho comprate **per lei**.   *I bought **them for her**.*

- Use the *double pronoun* construction, which is the more common: both the *direct object* and the *indirect object pronoun* are placed *before the verb*.

   Me lo hai portato.   *You brought **me it**.*
   Gliele ho comprate.   *I bought them **for her**.*

Double pronouns are composed of the weak forms of the direct object and the indirect object pronouns. The indirect object pronouns change their ending from **-i** to **-e**, to make pronunciation easier.

Combo forms {

me lo/la/li/le	him/her/it/them to me
te lo/la/li/le	him/her, etc., to you
glielo/gliela/glieli/gliele	him/her, etc., to him
glielo/gliela/glieli/gliele	him/her, etc., to her
ce lo/la/li/le	him/her, etc., to us
ve lo/la/li/le	him/her, etc., to you
glielo/a/li/le	him/her, etc., to them

Glie is used for the third person singular and plural, masculine and feminine. **Glie** + **lo/la/li/le** form one word.

> Porto **il libro a mia madre**.   *I'm taking **the book to my mother**.*
>
> Porto **il libro a mio padre**.   *I'm taking **the book to my father**.*

Le porto **il libro**.	*I'm taking the book to her.*
Gli porto **il libro**.	*I'm taking the book to him.*
Glielo porto.	*I'm taking it to her.*
Glielo porto.	*I'm taking it to him.*
Porto **il libro ai miei genitori**.	*I'm taking the book to my parents.*
Gli porto **il libro**.	*I'm taking the book to them.*
Glielo porto.	*I'm taking it to them.*

We use the *preposition + the strong form of the indirect object pronoun* when we wish to avoid confusion.

Glielo porto domani (ad Anna).	**Lo** porto **a lei** domani.	*I will take it to her tomorrow.*

Placement of Double Pronouns

In positive, negative, and interrogative sentences, *double pronouns* are placed *before the verb form*, and *between the negation and the verb*, like any other weak pronoun.

Glielo sto dicendo.	*I'm telling it to him.*
Non ve lo mandano?	*Don't they send it to you?*

esercizio	4-1

In the following sentences, replace nouns and names expressing the direct and indirect objects with the appropriate pronouns.

EXAMPLE: I'm telling that story to my father.   →   I'm telling it to him.

1. I'm giving the gift to my mother. _____

2. She's writing a letter to her brother. _____

3. We're opening the room for the senator. _____

4. You (*pl.*) are sending that photograph to their sisters. _____

_____

5. I'm preparing dinner for you (*sing.*). _____

6. You (*sing.*) are closing that account for me. _____

7. They're cleaning the box for her cat. (*fem.*) _____

8. He's showing the paintings to us. _____

9. She's delivering those messages to you. _____

esercizio 4-2

Translate the sentences using the simple present. Place the double pronoun before the verb.

        EXAMPLE: I'm telling that story to my father.   →   Gliela dico.

1. I'm giving the gift to my mother. _____

2. She's writing a letter to her brother. _____

3. We're opening the room for the senator. _____

4. You (*pl.*) are sending that photograph to their sisters. _____

5. I'm preparing dinner for you (*sing.*). _____

6. You (*sing.*) are closing that account for me. _____

7. They're cleaning the box for her cat. _____

8. He's showing the paintings to us. (*mostrare*) _____

9. She's delivering those messages to you (*pl*). _____

esercizio 4-3

In the following sentences, replace the nouns and names expressing the direct and indirect objects with the appropriate pronouns. Use to/for + indirect object pronouns.

        EXAMPLE: We don't send the package to Elsa.   →   We don't send it to her.

1. I'm building the desk for the children. _____

2. He doesn't mail the picture to me. _____

3. Will they open the store for you? _____

4. You're offering your help to Carlo. _____

5. I will give my book to Sara. _____

6. He's preparing the report for the directors. _____

7. You're preparing the meal for my friends and myself. _____

_____

8. They will explain the problem to you and your friends. _____

_____

Placement with the Imperative, the Infinitive, and the Gerund

When the verb is in the imperative (second person singular and plural), the infinitive, or the gerund, the double pronouns are attached to the verb.

Porta**melo**!	*Bring **it to me**!*
... portando**melo**.	*. . . (by) bringing **it to me**.*
Portar**melo**.	*To bring **it to me**.*

When we use the *strong* forms of the indirect object pronouns, the direct object is *attached to the verb*.

Porta**lo a me**!	*Bring **it to me**!*
... portando**lo a me**.	*. . . bringing **it to me**.*
... portar**lo a me**.	*. . . to bring **it to me**.*

esercizio   4-4

In the following sentences, replace the noun that forms the direct object and the indirect object pronoun with the appropriate double pronoun attached to the verb.

1. Manda il regalo a lei! _____

2. Impresta la tua macchina a loro! _____

3. Portate il telefono a noi! _____

4. Offrite un cioccolatino a lui! _____

5. Mostra le carte a me! _____

esercizio   4-5

In the following sentences, replace the nouns/names in italics that convey the direct and indirect objects with double pronouns, attaching them to the infinitive, the imperative, or the gerund.

1. Hai detto a Luigi di portare *le chiavi ad Elisa?* _____

2. Dando *quella informazione a me*, mi hai aiutato molto. _____

_____

3. Rendi *il pallone a Roberto*! _____

4. Pensano di mandare *i fiori a lei?* _____

5. Comprando *i biglietti per noi*, ci avete fatto un bel regalo. _____

_____

Placement with the Negative Form of the Imperative

With the negative form of the imperative (second person singular and plural), double pronouns can be either *attached to the verb* or *placed between the negation and the verb.*

Non portar**melo**!	***Don't*** *bring **it to me**!*
Non portate**cele**!	***Don't*** *bring **them to us**!*
Non me lo portare!	***Don't*** *bring **it to me**!*
Non ce le portate!	***Don't*** *bring **them to us**!*

When we use the *strong forms* of the indirect object pronoun, the latter will *follow the verb*. The direct object pronouns *can be attached to the imperative* or placed *between the negation and the verb.*

Non portar**lo a me**!	***Don't*** *bring **it to me**!*
Non portate**le a noi**!	***Don't*** *bring **them to us**!*
Non lo portare **a me**!	***Don't*** *bring **it to me**!*
Non le portate **a noi**!	***Don't*** *bring **them to us**!*

esercizio 4-6

Translate the following sentences, attaching the double pronouns to the verb.

1. Don't send the gift to her! _____

2. Don't lend your car to them! _____

3. Don't bring (*pl.*) the telephone to us! _____

4. Don't offer (*pl.*) wine to him! _____

5. Don't show the cards to me! (*mostrare*) _____

Double Pronouns with Compound Tenses

With the present perfect (e.g., *I have spoken*), the double pronouns are placed *before the verb form*. When the object pronoun precedes the past participle, the latter will be coordinated with the gender and number of the pronoun.

Ci ha raccontato **la tua storia**.	→	**Ce l(a)**'ha raccontata.
*He told **us your story**.*	→	He told ***it to us***.

With the *present progressive*, the *double pronouns* can either be placed *before the verb form* or *attached to the gerund*. (Remember that the gerund is invariable.)

Ci sta raccontando **la tua storia**.	→	**Ce la** sta raccontando. /
		Sta raccontando**cela**.
*He's telling **us your story**.*	→	He's telling ***it to us***.

With the past infinitive, the double pronouns can be *attached to the infinitive.*

Dice di aver dato **il pacco a loro**.   →   Dice di aver**glielo** dato.
*He says he gave **the package to him**.*   →   *He says he gave **it to him**.*

   **4-7**

In the following sentences, replace the simple present with the present progressive and the nouns/names with double pronouns placed before the verb form.

1. Dai l'automobile a Elena. _____

2. Portiamo il cane allo zio. _____

3. Preparano la festa per voi. _____

4. Mostrate il filmino a Enrico. _____

5. Costruisce la barca per te. _____

6. Indichiamo la strada agli ospiti. _____

7. Pittura la cucina per me. _____

esercizio   **4-8**

*Translate the following sentences using the double pronouns, **me lo**, **te la**, ecc., placed before the verb. Use the verbs suggested in parentheses. Remember that the past participle must be coordinated with the gender of the direct object when the latter precedes the verb.*

1. I built the desk for them. (*costruire*) _____

2. He mailed the photograph to me. (*spedire*) _____

3. They opened the store for you (*sing.*). (*aprire*) _____

4. You (*sing.*) offered your help to me. (*offrire*) _____

5. I'm giving the book to her. (*dare*) _____

6. He wrote the letters to them. (*scrivere*) _____

7. You (*pl.*) are preparing the meal for us. (*preparare*) _____

8. They explained the problem to you (*pl.*). (*spiegare*) _____

Placement with Modal Auxiliaries (*Verbi Servili*)

With the modal auxiliaries **dovere** (*must*), **potere** (*may/can*), **volere** (*will*), and **sapere** (*to know*) used as modifiers of another verb in the infinitive (e.g., *I can see, I must go*), the double pronoun can either be *attached to the infinitive* or placed *before the verb form*. There is no set rule about where to place the double pronouns.

> Posso mandar**vela**. ⎫
> **Ve la** posso mandare. ⎭   *I can send **it to you**.*

When we use the *strong forms* of the indirect object pronouns, the latter will *follow the verb*. The direct object pronouns *can be attached to the infinitive*, or be placed *before the verb form*.

> Posso mandar**la a voi**. ⎫
> **La** posso mandare **a voi**. ⎭   *I can send **it to you**.*

esercizio   4-9

Replace the nouns/name conveying the direct/indirect object with the double pronoun attached to the verb in the infinitive.

1. Voglio ricordare l'appuntamento a Massimo. _____

2. Devi raccontare la tua disavventura a tua sorella. _____

3. Sanno mandare i documenti all'avvocato. _____

4. Può comprare il gelato a te. _____

5. Volete promettere una ricompensa ai ragazzi? _____

6. Devo vendere il quadro a voi. _____

7. Vuole aprire la casa per me. _____

esercizio   4-10

Using the same sentences, place the double pronouns before the verb forms.

1. Voglio ricordare l'appuntamento a Massimo. _____

2. Devi raccontare la tua disavventura a tua sorella. _____

3. Sanno mandare i documenti all'avvocato. _____

4. Può comprare il gelato a te. _____

5. Volete promettere una ricompensa ai ragazzi? _____

6. Devo vendere il quadro a voi. _____

7. Vuole aprire la casa per me. _____

Answer the following questions in the affirmative, using the double pronouns attached to the verb in the infinitive.

1. Vuoi organizzare il viaggio per Marco? _____

2. Sanno aprire la cassaforte per me e i miei fratelli? _____

3. Posso affittare l'appartamento ai suoi amici? _____

4. Dovete vendere i gioielli a me? _____

5. Vogliamo comprare la sciarpa alla mamma? _____

6. Sai chiudere il conto per loro? _____

7. Devo scaricare il programma per voi? _____

8. Deve pagare l'affitto al padrone di casa? _____

9. Vuole offrire un brindisi a voi? _____

10. Sa dare la medicina alla bambina? _____

When the modal verb is followed by a *past infinitive*, double pronouns can either be *attached to the infinitive* or *placed before the verb form.*

Posso aver**vela** mandata. ⎫
Ve la posso aver mandata. ⎬ *I may have sent **it to you**.*

Replace the direct object and the indirect object with the appropriate double pronoun, attaching it to the infinitive.

1. Vorresti aver organizzato il viaggio per Marco? _____

2. Possono aver affittato l'appartamento ai loro amici. _____

3. Vorreste aver venduto i gioielli a me? _____

4. Dovrebbero aver finito il lavoro per la mamma. _____

5. Devono aver scaricato il programma per voi. _____

Causative Verbs (*Verbi Causativi*): *Lasciare, Fare*

With the causative verbs **lasciare** and **fare**, the double pronouns are placed *before the causative verbs* or *attached to them with the imperative, the gerund, and the infinitive.*

Me lo lascia fare.	*He lets **me** do **it**.*
Fate**gliela** vendere!	*Make **them** sell **it**!*

esercizio   **4-13**

Replace the strong form of the indirect object pronoun and the direct object with the corresponding double pronoun, either before the causative verb or attached to it when possible.

1. Fa finire a lei quel lavoro! _____

2. Ci lasciate portare il cane? _____

3. Non vi lasciano invitare quella ragazza. _____

4. Fate portare il cappotto al signore. _____

5. Lasci vedere la casa ai signori? _____

6. Mi lasciate vedere quel film? _____

7. Ti lasciano prendere a prestito la macchina. _____

Reflexive Pronouns and *Si* as Impersonal Pronoun

Reflexive pronouns convey the idea that the action expressed by the verb falls on the performer.

*I wash **my own person**.*	→	*I wash **myself**.*
*She weighs **her own person**.*	→	*She weighs **herself**.*

As reflexive pronouns, Italian uses the weak forms of the direct object pronouns *modified only in the third person singular and plural.*

Pronomi riflessivi (*Reflexive pronouns*)

mi	myself
ti	yourself
si	himself
si	herself
si	itself
si	oneself
ci	ourselves
vi	yourselves
si	themselves

The reflexive pronouns are placed *before the verb* like any other weak pronoun.

Io mi lavo.	*I'm washing **myself**.*
Vi pulite?	*Are you cleaning **yourselves**?*

In Italian, more verbs take the reflexive forms than in English—for example, verbs that express care of the body. Here are the most important reflexive verbs:

A. Care of the Body

asciugarsi	to dry oneself
cambiarsi	to change one's clothes
coprirsi	to cover oneself
lavarsi	to wash oneself
pesarsi	to weigh oneself

pettinarsi	to comb one's hair
pulirsi	to clean oneself
radersi	to shave
spazzolarsi (i capelli)	to brush one's hair
spogliarsi/svestirsi	to get undressed/to take one's clothes off
truccarsi	to make oneself up
vestirsi	to get dressed

esercizio   5-1

Translate the following sentences, choosing among the verbs listed under A. Translate all present progressive tenses with the simple present.

1. She weighs herself every day. _____

2. He shaves twice a day. _____

3. You (*pl.*) are making yourselves up for the show. _____

4. They're taking their clothes off. _____

5. The cat is washing herself. _____

6. My mother brushes her hair every evening. _____

7. I cover myself when it's cold. _____

8. Are you (*sing.*) getting dressed? _____

9. We're getting undressed. _____

Placement with the Imperative (Second Person Singular and Plural), the Infinitive, and the Gerund

Like any other weak pronoun, reflexive pronouns are attached to a *gerund*, an *imperative*, and *any infinitive* (e.g., **Lavandomi. Lavatevi!** Ho detto a Giulia di **lavarsi**. Devono **lavarsi**.).

esercizio   5-2

Translate the following sentences.

1. Comb (*sing.*) your hair! _____

2. I must get changed. _____

3. I will tell her (*simple pres.*) to wash herself. _____

4. Cover yourselves! _____

5. Don't weigh yourself again! _____

6. Can she dry herself? _____

7. They must clean themselves. _____

Compound Tenses

When the verb takes the reflexive form, the auxiliary verb is **essere** (*to be*). The *past participle* is coordinated with *the subject in gender and number.*

> **Si** è lavat**a**.   *She washed **herself**.*
> **Si** sono guardat**i** nello specchio.   ***They** looked at **themselves** in the mirror.*

Modal verbs in a compound tense followed by a reflexive verb can take **avere** or **essere** as their auxiliary.

> **Avrebbe dovuto lavarsi** → **Si sarebbe dovuto lavare**   *He should have washed*
>   le mani!   le mani!   *his hands!*
> **Ha voluto vestirsi** da sola. → **Si è voluta vestire** da sola.   *She wanted to get dressed*
>   *by herself.*

| esercizio | 5-3 |

Translate the following sentences. The ending of the past participle must be coordinated with the subject. The default is masculine.

1. She weighed herself a week ago. _____

2. When did he shave? _____

3. They made themselves up for the show. _____

4. You (*pl.*) took your clothes off! _____

5. The cat (*fem.*) washed herself. _____

6. I (*masc.*) covered myself well. _____

7. Why did you (*sing.*) uncover yourself (*masc.*)? _____

With the present progressive, the reflexive pronoun can be either placed *before the verb form* or *attached to the gerund.* The gerund does not change ending.

> Maria **si** sta lavando. Maria sta lavando**si**.   *Maria is washing **herself**.*
> **Vi** state pettinando? / State pettinando**vi**?   *Are you combing **your hair**?*

Reflexive Pronouns and Direct Objects

Many verbs that take the direct object *also take the reflexive pronoun* to make it clear that the action falls on the subject. English usually adds the possessive to the direct object.

> Lavo **le mani**.

Question: **Whose** hands am I washing?

> Lavo le mani **a mia figlia**.   *I'm washing **my daughter's hands**.*

but

> **Mi** lavo **le mani**.   *I'm washing **my hands**.*

Most verbs used to talk about one's body and articles of clothing take both the direct and reflexive pronouns.

B. Body Parts and Articles of Clothing

asciugarsi gli occhi, il viso, la faccia, le mani, ecc.	to dry one's face, hands, etc.
cambiarsi il vestito, i pantaloni, ecc.	to change one's dress, trousers, etc.
coprirsi le mani, la testa, ecc.	to cover one's hands, head, etc.
farsi la barba, le unghie, ecc.	to shave/to polish one's nails, etc.
lavarsi le mani, la faccia, la testa, ecc.	to wash one's hands, face, head, etc.
lucidarsi le scarpe	to polish one's shoes
mettersi le calze, la maglia, ecc.	to put on stockings, pullover, etc.
pettinarsi i capelli	to comb one's hair
pulirsi la faccia, le mani, le unghie	to clean one's face, hands, nails, etc.
scoprirsi la testa, le gambe, ecc.	to uncover one's head, legs, etc.
spazzolarsi i capelli, ecc.	to brush one's hair
togliersi il cappotto, i pantaloni, ecc.	to take off one's coat, pants, etc.
truccarsi, ecc.	to make up one's eyes, face, etc.

esercizio   5-4

Translate the following sentences, choosing among the verbs from lists A and B. Use the simple present to translate the present progressive.

1. She likes to brush her hair. (*piacere + inf.*) _____

2. Clean (*pl.*) your face! _____

3. He combs his hair, but does not shave. _____

4. We had (*abbiamo dovuto*) to change our socks after the game. _____

_____

5. They are making up their faces. _____

6. Are you (*sing.*) shaving? _____

7. We cover our heads in church. _____

Doing Things for Oneself

The reflexive is also used to convey the idea that *one is doing something for oneself,* even though the action does not fall on the subject.

      Mi cucino **una bella cena.**

does not mean

      *I cook **myself for dinner.***

It means

      *I'm cooking **a nice dinner for myself.** / I'm cooking **myself a nice dinner.***

Here follows a list of verbs often used when doing things for oneself.

C. Doing Things for Oneself

ascoltarsi	to listen to
bersi	to drink
comprarsi	to buy
costruirsi	to build
cucinarsi	to cook
cucirsi	to saw
farsi	to do
giocarsi (more often meaning "to lose")	to gamble (*away*)
leggersi	to read
mangiarsi	to eat
prepararsi	to prepare
stirarsi	to iron
vendersi	to sell

esercizio 5-5

Add the appropriate reflexive pronoun to the following sentences. Attach the pronoun to the verb whenever possible.

    EXAMPLE: Costruisce una bella casa.   →   Si costruisce una bella casa.

1. Compro un abito da sera lungo. _____

2. Volete cucinare un arrosto? _____

3. Non bevete tutta la bottiglia! _____

4. Elena ha intenzione di giocare 1.000.000,00 euro alla roulette. _____

_____

5. Mio marito stira le camicie. _____

6. Prepariamo le valigie. _____

7. Vendono tutte le azioni. _____

Coordination of the Reflexive Pronoun with the Auxiliary and the Past Participle

A verb that takes a direct object usually takes the auxiliary **avere**. However, when there is a reflexive pronoun, the verb takes the auxiliary **essere**.

| Anna ha cambiato l'abito. | → | Anna **si** è cambiata l'abito. | *Anna changed her dress.* |

When the direct object *follows* the past participle, the past participle is *coordinated with the subject in gender and number.* The default gender is masculine.

Le suore si sono lavate **le mani.**   *The nuns washed their hands.*
I calciatori si sono lavati **le mani.**   *The soccer players washed their hands.*

esercizio   5-6

*In the following sentences, change the auxiliary from **avere** to **essere** and add the appropriate reflexive pronoun.*

EXAMPLE: Ida ha spazzolato i capelli.   →   Ida si è spazzolata i capelli.

1. I bambini non hanno pulito le unghie. _____

2. Mia nonna non ha pettinato bene i capelli. _____

3. Avete coperto la testa? _____

4. Nicola ha cambiato i pantaloni. _____

5. Ho messo (*fem.*) le calze. _____

6. Tolga pure il cappotto, Signora. _____

7. Le mie sorelle hanno truccato solo gli occhi. _____

8. Gli attori hanno truccato tutto il viso. _____

9. Il nonno ha fatto la barba? _____

10. Abbiamo lavato (*masc.*) le mani. _____

Reciprocal Reflexive Verbs (*Verbi Riflessivi Reciproci*)

Italian uses the reflexive form when two or more people perform an action that affects *all subjects reciprocally.* English often uses the phrases *each other* or *one another.*

Loro due si amano.	*Those two love each other.*
Ci siamo guardati.	*We looked at one another.*
Angela e Rita si sono abbracciate.	*Angela and Rita embraced.*
Vi assomigliate molto!	*You really look alike!*

Reciprocal reflexive verbs can be used by a singular subject reflexively—**Si guarda** allo specchio. (*He's looking at himself in the mirror.*)—or by a plural subject reciprocally—**Si guardano** attraverso la sala. (***They are looking at each other*** *across the room.*).

D. Reciprocal Reflexive Verbs

abbracciarsi	to embrace each other
aiutarsi	to help each other
amarsi	to love each other
assomigliarsi	to look alike
baciarsi	to kiss each other
capirsi	to understand (each other)
chiamarsi	to give a call to/to call each other
conoscersi	to know/to get acquainted with each other
desiderarsi	to desire each other
dividersi	to split/to separate
evitarsi	to avoid each other
fidanzarsi	to get engaged
guardarsi	to look at each other
incontrarsi	to meet (each other)
innamorarsi	to fall in love with each other
lasciarsi	to leave each other
odiarsi	to hate each other
parlarsi	to talk (to each other)
presentarsi	to introduce each to the other
riconoscersi	to recognize each other
scambiarsi (*indirizzo, numero di telefono, ecc.*)	to exchange (*addresses, telephone numbers,* etc.)
scriversi	to write to each other
spiegarsi	to explain
sposarsi	to get married
telefonarsi	to ring/to call each other
toccarsi	to touch each other
tradirsi	to betray each other
vedersi/incontrarsi	to see each other/to meet
venirsi incontro	to come half way
volersi bene	to love/care for each other

esercizio   5-7

Translate the following sentences. Use the simple present to convey both the near future and the present progressive.

1. Franca and Nicoletta care for one another. _____

2. Massimo and Luciana are getting married. _____

3. Shall we call one another tomorrow? _____

4. My brothers help one another a lot. _____

5. We understand each other. _____

6. Olga and I write to one another. _____

7. They will see each other tomorrow. _____

8. They got separated after twenty years of marriage. _____

esercizio   5-8

Translate the following sentences. Use the present perfect.

1. Franca and Nicoletta have always cared for each other. _____

   _____

2. Massimo and Luciana got married a year ago. _____

3. We exchanged telephone numbers. _____

4. My brothers have always helped one another a lot. _____

5. We never understood each other. _____

6. Olga and I (*fem.*) have written long letters to one another for many years. _____

   _____

7. They saw one another a week ago. _____

8. They embraced. _____

Reflexive Verbs and Direct Object Pronouns

A reflexive verb can take a *reflexive pronoun **and** a direct object pronoun*, which can form a double pronoun. To make pronunciation easier, the reflexive pronoun changes the ending from **-i** to **-e**. The same pronoun is used for the third person singular and plural.

«**Si** cucina **la cena**»? «**Se la** cucina».	*"Is she cooking **dinner for herself**?" "She is."*
«**Ti** compri **quelle scarpe**»? «**Me** le compro».	*"Will you buy **those shoes**?" "I will buy **them**."*

Pronomi riflessivi + Complemento oggetto	(*Reflexive + Direct object pronouns*)
me + lo/la/li/le	it/them for/to myself
te + lo/la/li/le	it/them for/to yourself
se + lo/la/li/le	it/them for/to him/herself
ce + lo/la/li/le	it/them for/to ourselves
ve + lo/la/li/le	it/them for/to yourselves
se + lo/la/li/le	it/them for/to themselves

Placement

With most finite tenses, double pronouns are placed *before the verb*. With the *imperative*, the *gerund*, and the *infinitive*, double pronouns can form one word, attached to the verb. With *modal auxiliaries* followed by an infinitive, double pronouns can be placed either *before the modal verb* or *after the infinitive*.

Mi cambio **le scarpe**.	→	**Me le** cambio.
*I'm changing **my shoes**.*	→	*I'm changing **them**.*
Compra**ti** una giacca!	→	Compra**tela**!
*Buy yourself **a coat**!*	→	*Buy **it**!*
Gianna sta lavando**si** i denti.	→	Gianna sta lavando**seli**.
*She's brushing **her** teeth.*	→	*She's brushing **them**.*
Potrei legger**mi** quel bel libro.	→	Potrei legger**melo**.
*I could read **that nice book**.*	→	*I could read **it**.*

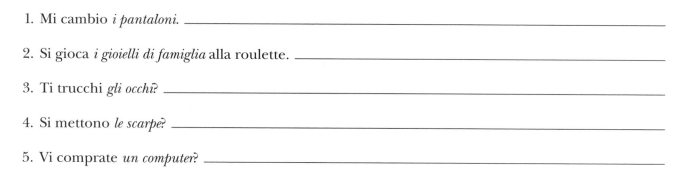

esercizio   5-9

Replace the nouns in italics with direct object pronouns. Place the reflexive pronoun + direct object pronoun before the verb.

1. Mi cambio *i pantaloni*. _____

2. Si gioca *i gioielli di famiglia* alla roulette. _____

3. Ti trucchi *gli occhi*? _____

4. Si mettono *le scarpe*? _____

5. Vi comprate *un computer*? _____

Double Pronouns: Coordination with the Past Participle

When the tense of the verb requires a past participle and the direct object pronoun precedes the verb, the *past participle* is coordinated with the *direct object pronoun* (as happens when the auxiliary is **avere**).

Si è lavat**o le mani**?	→	**Se le** è lavat**e**?
*Did he wash **his hands**?*	→	Did he wash **them**?

When there is a modal auxiliary followed by a verb in a past tense, the double pronoun can be either placed *before the modal auxiliary* or *attached to the infinitive*.

Deve esser**si** lavat**a le mani**.   ***She** must have washed **her hands**.*
Se le dev'essere lavat**e**. /   ***She** must have washed **them**.*
      Dev'esser**sele** lavat**e**.

---

esercizio   5-10

Replace the nouns in italics with the direct object pronouns. The reflexive + direct object pronouns either are placed before the verb or are attached to the infinitive.

1. Ti sei preparata *le valigie?* _____

2. Si sono tolti *il casco.* _____

3. Devono essersi lucidati *le scarpe.* _____

4. Ci siamo coperte *il capo.* _____

5. Vi siete asciugati *le mani?* _____

6. Si è cambiata *il maglione.* _____

7. Mi sono tolta *il cappotto.* _____

8. Si è cucinato *la bistecca.* _____

Si as Impersonal Pronoun

English conveys an impersonal subject through the words *one, we, you, they, people*.

***One** always thinks other people are more interesting.*
***One/You** should never give people advice.*
***They** don't like strangers around here.*
***They/People** say her husband is divorcing her.*

In Italian we can use **tu/voi, loro,** and **la gente**. But the most commonly used impersonal pronoun is the pronoun **si**, which is used to generalize about an indefinite group of people that may or may not include the subject.

Si parla di indire elezioni anticipate.	**There is talk** of calling the elections before the end of the mandate.
Si va al cinema stasera?	**Shall we** go to the movies tonight?
Non **si** può imparare una lingua straniera in sei settimane.	**One/You** can't learn a foreign language in six weeks.

Si + *verb in the third person singular* can be used with most verbs, in all modes and tenses. With a compound tense, the auxiliary will be **essere**; the past participle will take the *masculine*. Impersonal verbs, such as **bisogna** (*it is necessary*), **conviene** (*it is better/advantageous*), **importa/non importa** (*it matters/it doesn't matter*), **piove** (*it rains/it's raining*), **sembra** (*it seems*), and **succede** (*it happens*), cannot take the reflexive form.

Si è parlato di Mario al bar.	**People** talked about Mario in the bar.
Si è mangiato molto al matrimonio.	**The guests** ate a lot at the wedding.

---

esercizio   5-11

Translate the following sentences.

1. Si pensa che ci sarà un altro attacco terroristico. _____

   _____

2. Ragazzi, si parte alle sei domattina! _____

3. Si impara più in fretta quando si è giovani. _____

4. Si dice che il principe sposerà una straniera. Si vedrà. _____

   _____

5. Si mangia bene in quel ristorante. _____

6. Si è parlato molto di vendere la ditta. _____

7. Si lavora troppo al giorno d'oggi. _____

8. Si gioca a golf, domenica? _____

---

esercizio   5-12

*Translate the following sentences. Use **si** + the third person singular.*

1. We give too little financial aid to poor countries. _____

   _____

2. One believes (*credere*) the mass media too much. _____

3. One doesn't believe (*credere a*) the politicians. _____

_____

4. We are dying from hunger! _____

5. We are thinking of (*pensare di*) selling the house. _____

_____

6. It is said that he wants (*voglia*) to become president. _____

_____

7. You can play poker in that club. _____

8. You don't want to bet on the stock market now. _____

_____

Note: When the impersonal pronoun **si** is used with a reflexive verb, the reflexive pronoun will be **ci** rather than **si.**

Ci si lava le mani.	*We wash our hands.*
	One washes one's hands.
Ci si sveglia alle sette.	*We wake up at 7 A.M.*
	One wakes up at 7 A.M.

The Pronoun *Ne*

Ne is an invariable pronoun (weak form). It can replace masculine, feminine, and neuter antecedents. **Ne** plays several functions.

Ne (of/by Someone/Something)

Ne can be used as an indirect object pronoun, meaning *of him/her/them*, and *by him/her/them*.

>   «Ho appena visto **Carla**...» «Non mi parlare **di lei**»!
>   «Non me **ne** parlare»!

>   means

>   "I just saw **Carla** . . ."   "Don't talk to me **about her!**"

>   Non **la** conosce bene, ma è affascinato **da lei**.
>   Non **la** conosce bene, ma **ne** è affascinato.

>   means

>   He doesn't know **her** well, but he's fascinated **by her**.

Ne also takes the place of the possessive, which in Italian is conveyed through *the preposition* **di** + *the noun conveying the owner,* or by *the possessive adjective + a noun.*

>   Apprezzo l'intelligenza **di Carlo**.
>   **Ne** apprezzo l'intelligenza.

>   means

>   *I appreciate **Carlo's** intelligence.*

>   Apprezzo **la sua** intelligenza.
>   **Ne** apprezzo l'intelligenza.

>   means

>   *I appreciate **his** intelligence.*

Placement of *Ne*

Ne behaves like any other *weak pronoun*. It is placed *before the verb* in most finite forms and *between* the particle **non** and the verb in negative clauses. It can be attached to the *infinitive*, the *gerund*, and the *imperative*.

Sentendo**ne** parlare tanto,
    ha voluto conoscer**li**.
Hanno conosciuto Lucia. Adesso
    vorrebbero conoscer**ne i genitori**.
	*Having heard so much **about them**,
	    he wanted to meet **them**.*
	*They met Lucia. Now they would
	    like to meet **her parents**.*

esercizio	6-1

*In the following sentences, replace the words in italics with the pronoun **ne**. Place the pronoun before the verb.*

1. Ho sentito parlare *di lui.* _____

2. Sai qualcosa *di loro?* _____

3. Apprezzo il senso dell'umorismo *di Marta.* _____

4. Conoscete i genitori *dei vostri amici?* _____

5. È rimasto colpito *da Bianca.* _____

6. Ricordi il nome *dell'ingegnere?* _____

7. È la baby-sitter *di quella bambina.* _____

8. Abbiamo una buona opinione *del nuovo collega.* _____

Ne (of This, of That/from This, from That)

Ne can replace a phrase or a concept already expressed—**di ciò, di questo, di quello; da questo, da quello** (*of it, about it, of this, of that, by/from this, by/from that*), etc. It can also refer to an entire sentence.

Hanno dicusso **della questione**.	→	**Ne** hanno discusso.
*They talked **about that issue**.*	→	*They talked **about it**.*

Deduco **dalle tue parole** che non
    le credi.
Ne deduco che non le credi.
«Dicono **che dia le dimissioni**».
    «**Ne** sai qualcosa»?
	*I infer **from your words** that you don't
	    believe her.*
	*I infer **from that** that you don't believe her.*
	*"They say **he will quit**."*
	    *"Do you know anything **about it**?"*

---

esercizio	6-2

In the following sentences, replace the words in italics with the pronoun **ne**.

1. Ho parlato a mio padre *dell'incidente.* _____

2. Non sapeva niente *del premio.* _____

3. Abbiamo una pessima opinione *del lavoro di restauro.* _____

_____

4. Non vedono la necessità *di chiedere un altro prestito.* _____

_____

5. Vale la pena *lavorare tanto?* _____

6. Non riuscite a fare a meno *di fumare?* _____

Ne as Partitive Pronoun (*Pronome Partitivo*)

The antecedent of **ne** can be a *countable or uncountable whole* of which we can specify *a part or quantity.* When **ne** plays this function, it is called **pronome partitivo**.

Ne is usually accompanied by a word indicating the quantity/part of the whole.

«Mangi **la carne**»?	*"Do you eat **meat**?"*
«**Ne** mangio **un pezzetto**».	*"I will eat **a piece**."*
«Vuoi **delle mele**»?	*"Do you want **any apples**?"*
«**Ne** voglio **una**».	*"I want **one**."*

But **ne** can also be used by itself, leaving implicit the word conveying the part.

«Mangi **la carne**»? «Non **ne** mangio».   *"Do you eat **meat**?" "I don't."*

Words conveying quantity

uno/una, due, tre, quattro... cinquantacinque, novantotto, ecc.	1, 2, 3, 4 . . . 55, 98, etc.
1 chilo, due etti, tre chilometri, ecc.	*1 kilo, 200 grams, 3 kilometers, etc.*
Abbastanza	*Enough*
Del/dello, dei/degli, della/delle	*A little, some, any*

Many indefinite pronouns convey quantity. For a list, see Unit 12.

Del/dello, della, ecc., are formed by joining the preposition **di** (*of*) and the definite articles **il/lo, la**, ecc., (see Unit 13), they may mean *of the*, or *a little, some*. When **del/dello, della**, ecc., mean *of the*, they help us to add information about someone or something, or to indicate possession.

Quel libro parla **della guerra**.   *That book talks **about the war**.*
Il cane **di Paolo** è simpatico.   ***Paolo's dog** is nice.*

When they are used as indefinite articles, **del/dello**, **della**, ecc., mean *a little, some.*

Vuoi **della coca-cola**?   *Would you like **some coke**?*
Vorrei **della carne**.   *I would like **some meat**.*

In both cases, the pronoun **ne** can be used to replace the antecedent introduced by the preposition **di** or the indefinite article **del/dello/della**, ecc.

Quel libro **ne parla**.   *That book talks **about it**.*
Ne vorrei.   *I'd like **some**.*

esercizio   6-3

*In the following sentences, decide whether **del, dei,** ecc., means a little, some, or of the.*

	a little/some	of the
1. Vuoi della birra?	———	———
2. Ti ricordi di Anna?	———	———
3. Mangiate del pesce?	———	———
4. Parliamo del film?	———	———
5. Vendete delle pesche?	———	———
6. Non volete del riso?	———	———
7. Vuoi mezzo chilo di riso?	———	———

esercizio   6-4

*In the following sentences, replace the nouns/names in italics with the pronoun **ne**. Exclamation marks indicate that the verb is in the imperative. Attach **ne** to the imperative or the infinitive. If there is a word/phrase conveying a specific quantity, repeat it in the sentence with **ne**.*

1. Bevo *del vino.* _____

2. Rivedranno tre *dei loro cugini* a Natale. _____

3. Compriamo *del pane.* _____

4. Vendono una *delle lore barche.* _____

5. Vogliono noleggiare *uno di quei film.* _____

6. Prendete *uno di quegli ombrelli?* _____

7. Spedite *una di quelle cartoline* a vostra zia! _____

8. Cogliete *dieci di quelle piante!* _____

9. Vogliono regalare *mille dei loro libri* alla biblioteca pubblica. _____

_____

10. Non mette *zucchero* nel caffè. _____

Ne and Gender/Number Coordination

In a sentence where the verb contains a past participle (**aver mangiato**, **aver comprato**, ecc.) and the pronoun **ne**, the past participle must be coordinated with the *gender and number of the antecedent* to which **ne** refers.

«Hai comprato **dei pomodori**»?	*"Did you buy **any tomatoes**?"*
«Sì, ne ho **comprati**».	*"Yes, I bought **some**."*
«Ha mangiato **delle mele**»?	*"Did she eat **any apples**?"*
«Sì, **ne** ha mangiat**e**».	*"Yes, she ate **some**."*

When the sentence contains the words **uno/nessuno** (*one/no one*), the past participle will take *the singular* and will be coordinated in *gender* with the antecedent.

«Hai comprato **dei pomodori**»?	*"Did you buy **any tomatoes**?"*
«No, non **ne** ho comprato **nessuno**».	*"No, I didn't buy **any**."*
«Ha mangiato **delle mele**»?	*"Did she eat **any apples**?"*
«No, non **ne** ha mangiat**a** **nessuna**».	*No, she did **not** eat **any**."*

esercizio 6-5

*Translate the following sentences. Use **del/dello**, **della**, ecc., to convey an indefinite quantity before a noun.*

1. "Did you (*pl.*) buy some zucchini?" "Yes, I bought (some)."

_____

2. "Did they take any sandwiches?" "Yes, they took five."

_____

3. "Did you (*sing.*) eat any chocolates?" "Yes, I ate one."

_____

4. "Did you eat any peaches?" "Yes, I ate one."

_____

5. "Did you (*pl.*) drink enough water?" "Yes, I drank enough."

_____

6. "Did she find any interesting recipes?" "Yes, she found three."

_____

7. "Did you see any good films?" "No, I didn't see any."

_____

8. "Did you see any nice skirts?" "No, I didn't see any."

_____

Ne and Double Pronouns

Ne can be coupled with the indirect object pronouns seen in Unit 3, forming the double pronouns **me ne, te ne, gliene, ce ne, ve ne, gliene**.

Me ne ha parlato ieri.	*He talked **to me about it** yesterday.*
Ve ne hanno detto qualcosa?	*Did they tell **you** anything **about that**?*

Rules for placement are the same as for the other double pronouns. **Gliene** can be used for the third person singular and plural, masculine and feminine.

Depending on the tense and mood of the verb, **ne** can be either placed before the verb or attached to it.

Gliene ho parlato ieri. (*ad Anna*)	*I talked **about it to her** yesterday.*
Parle**gliene**!	*Talk **to her about it**!*

esercizio   **6-6**

*Replace the names/nouns conveying to whom the action is addressed (**bold**) with indirect object pronouns. Replace the thing of which we are specifying a part (in italics) with **ne**. Attach the double pronoun to the verb when possible.*

1. Ho portato *della torta* **a Oscar**. _____

2. Abbiamo comprato *del gelato* **per la mamma**. _____

3. Hai comprato *del pane* **per noi**? _____

4. Avete venduto *delle mele* **a Donatella**? _____

5. Non ha mandato nessun *messaggio* **a te**? _____

6. Devono aver imprestato *una macchina* **a mio fratello**. _____

_____

7. Ho preso *dei soldi in banca* **per te**. _____

8. Volete comprare *una bicicletta* **per me**? _____

esercizio   **6-7**

*Replace the names/nouns conveying to whom the action is addressed (**bold**) with weak indirect object pronouns; and use **ne** to indicate the person/thing of whom/which we are talking (in italics). **Ne** is used here to mean of someone and of this/that. Remember that **ne** can refer to an entire phrase or sentence.*

1. Abbiamo parlato *di Gianna* **ai suoi genitori**. _____

2. Ha parlato **a me** *della sua fidanzata*. _____

3. Ho riferito **a lui** *della vostra scoperta*. _____

4. Hanno dato **a noi** buone informazioni *su di lui*. _____

_____

Ne and Reflexive Pronouns

Ne can also be coupled with the *reflexive pronouns* to form the double pronouns **me ne, te ne, se ne, ce ne, ve ne, se ne**. These are used with verbs that take the *reflexive form* together with:

A *direct object* that can be conveyed through the partitive pronoun **ne**.

> **Si** è comprata **tre gonne**.   }   *She bought **three skirts for herself**.*
> **Se ne** è comprate **tre**.

An *indirect object* introduced by the prepositions **di/da**.

> **Ci** occupiamo noi **di quel problema**.   **Ce ne** occupiamo noi.
> *We will take care **of that problem**.*   *We will take care of it.*

esercizio   **6-8**

*Replace the direct object (in italics) with the pronoun **ne** and form double pronouns with the reflexive pronouns (**bold**). Follow the rules of coordination given under "**Ne** and Gender/Number Coordination."*

1. **Mi** cucino uno *dei polli* **per me**. _____

2. **Si** comprano una parte *del terreno*. _____

3. **Si** trucca solo un *occhio?* _____

4. **Ti** prepari una *valigia?* _____

5. **Vi** bevete tre *Martini?* _____

6. **Si** fanno cinque *uova al tegamino!* _____

There are many verbs in Italian that take the *reflexive form* and an *indirect object* introduced by **di**. The indirect object can be a name, a noun, a sentence, or a pronoun.

Di + *the indirect object* becomes **ne**, which is used to form the double pronouns: **me ne, te ne,** ecc.

Mi sono dimenticato **di loro.**	→	**Me ne** sono dimenticato.	→	*I forgot **them**.*
Si sono pentiti **di averla calunniata.**	→	**Se ne** sono pentiti.	→	*They regretted **having slandered her**.*
				or
				*They **regretted it**.*

Reflexive verbs + *di*

accontentarsi di	to make do
accorgersi di	to become aware, to realize
allontanarsi da	to move away from
dimenticarsi di	to forget
innamorarsi di	to fall in love with
interessarsi di	to show interest for
liberarsi di	to get rid of
occuparsi di	to take care of
pentirsi di	to regret, to be sorry for
spaventarsi di	to become/get afraid of
stancarsi di	to get tired of
valersi di	to rely on, to take advantage of
vantarsi di	to boast about
vergognarsi di	to be ashamed of

Note. Verbs of motion such as **allontanarsene, andarsene, partirsene, venirsene, scapparsene, starsene,** ecc., take the reflexive forms and the particle **ne**, meaning *from that place.* When **andarsene** and **venirsene** are used alone they mean the same as **andare** and **venire.**

Si è allontanato **da lei?**	*Did he distance himself **from her**?*
Se ne è allontanato.	*He did.*
Me ne vado.	*I'm leaving.*
Te ne vai a passeggio da solo?	*Are you taking a stroll all by yourself?*

esercizio   **6-9**

*Replace the **bold** words with the reflexive pronoun and the words in italics with the pronoun **ne**. In compound tenses, coordinate the past participle in gender and number with the subject.*

1. **Ti** sei innamorato *di Franca?* _____

2. **Ci** interessiamo *del suo problema.* _____

3. **Vi** siete dimenticati *di avvisarlo?* _____

4. **Si** sono liberati *di quel seccatore di Filippo.* _____

5. La mia amica **si** è vergognata *delle sue parole.* _____

6. Dario **si** è stancato *di lei.* _____

7. **Mi** sono stancata *delle sue continue lamentele.* _____

8. **Vi** siete pentiti *di averlo abbandonato?* _____

9. Non **si** interessa più *di amministrare il patrimonio di sua madre.* _____

_____

Pronouns as Objects of Prepositions

As seen, we can omit prepositions when we use indirect object pronouns to answer the question to/for whom and when we use the pronoun **ne**. But when we use pronouns to convey other indirect objects, *we usually need to add a preposition.*

I work **with them**.	*Lavoro **con loro**.*
The portrait was painted **by her**.	*Il ritratto è stato dipinto **da lei**.*

The proposition is always followed by *the strong form of the object pronouns*. There are no corresponding weak forms.

Complementi indiretti a/con/per	(*Indirect objects*) (*at/to/with/for*) etc.
me	me
te	you
lui	him
lei/Lei	her/you (form.)
esso/essa	it
noi	us
voi/Voi	you
loro/Loro, **essi/esse**	them

Esso/essa, essi/esse are used for things and animals. They are used almost exclusively in writing.

Lei/Voi and **Loro** are used in addressing people and now often animals, especially pets.

Placement

In Italian, the placement of an indirect object formed by a *preposition + a pronoun* is very flexible. The most common placement is: (subject) + verb + (direct object) + preposition + indirect object pronoun.

Finisco la serata **da loro**.	*I will spend the rest of the evening **at their place**.*
Vado a cena **con lui**.	*I'm going out for dinner **with him**.*
Dicono belle cose **di lei**.	*They're saying nice things **about her**.*
Non sono contenti **di noi**.	*They are not happy **with our performance**.*

Indirect objects can also be placed before the verb; they can be inserted between the verb and the direct object, and between the verb and another indirect object. This holds for simple and compound tenses. Only context and style will dictate what position is appropriate.

Di voi mi fido.	*I trust **you**.*
Vado **con loro** in barca.	*I'm going sailing **with them**.*

With a negative sentence, indirect objects are placed either *before the negation* or *after the verb*.

Da te non è andato nessuno.	*No one went **to your place**.*
Non potevi fare di più **per lei**.	*You couldn't do anything else **for her**.*

The following, however, are incorrect and meaningless.

Non **da te** è andato nessuno.	*No one went to **your place**.*
Penso **da lei** di poter passare.	*I think I can stop by **at her place**.*
Non **con lui** ballate!	*Do not dance **with him**!*
Sta **da lei** andando.	*She is going **to her place**.*

esercizio   7-1

In the following sentences, replace the noun/names in italics with the appropriate indirect object pronouns. Use the prepositions suggested in parentheses. (For a full account of the use of prepositions, see Part II.)

1. Gioco a carte *con te e i tuoi cugini.* _____

2. *Da Franca* non abbiamo ricevuto niente. _____

3. Ho affidato tutti i miei affari *a mio cognato.* _____

4. Si fida totalmente *di sua madre.* _____

5. *Tra Paolo e Dario* ci sono sempre discussioni. _____

6. Passiamo *dalla zia?* (*da*) _____

7. Quella fotografia è stata presa *da Michele.* _____

8. Scrivo un libro *su Marilyn Monroe.* (*su di*) _____

esercizio	7-2

Translate the following sentences, using the prepositions suggested in parentheses.

1. He talks to them every day. (*con*) _____

2. Olga doesn't work for him. (*per*) _____

3. Are you (*sing.*) going to her place? (*da*) _____

4. She lives above me. (*sopra di*) _____

5. He must choose between you and me. (*tra*) _____

6. The dinner was prepared by him. (*da*) _____

7. We count on you (*sing.*). (*su di*) _____

Interrogative Pronouns

Interrogative pronouns allow us to acquire specific information about a person or a thing. In both Italian and English, they are used to introduce either a principal or a dependent clause. In either case they are placed at the beginning of the sentence they introduce.

Chi viene a cena?	***Who*** *is coming for dinner?*
Indovina **chi** viene a cena.	*Guess **who** is coming for dinner.*
Che cosa stai facendo?	***What*** *are you doing?*
Dimmi **che cosa** stai facendo.	Tell me **what** you're doing.

Pronomi interrogativi	(*Interrogative pronouns*)
chi	who/whom
di chi	whose
a/per/da chi	to/for/by, etc., whom
che/che cosa	what
quale/quali	what/which
quanto/a/i/e	how much/many

Chi? (Who?/Whom?)

Chi is used only for *people or animals*, especially pets, never for things. It is *invariable in gender and number* and is used both as *subject* and *direct object*. **Chi** is placed at the beginning of a clause, including in a negative clause.

Chi chiama?	***Who*** *is calling?*
Chi stai chiamando?	***Whom*** *are you calling?*
Chi non viene?	***Who*** *is not coming?*
Chi non hai invitato?	***Whom*** *didn't you invite?*
Vorrei sapere **chi** sta chiamando.	*I'd like to know **who** is calling.*
Non so **chi** stai chiamando.	*I don't know **whom** you're calling.*

Chi as Subject

When **chi** is used as subject, the verb takes the *third person singular*.

Chi lavora qui?	**Who** *works here?*
Chi va a scuola?	**Who** *is going to school?*

When the question regards the *identity* of a person or of a group of people, we use the verb **essere**, which *is coordinated with the person about whom we are inquiring*, if the sentence gives you sufficient clues. When we do not know who the person may be we say, "**Chi è?**" with no pronoun following the verb. English adds *it*.

Chi è?	*Who is it?*
Chi sono?	*Who are they?*
Chi sei tu?	*Who are you?*
Chi siamo noi?	*Who are we?*

esercizio	8-1

Translate the following questions.

1. Who is she? _____

2. Who doesn't want coffee? _____

3. Who are they? _____

4. Who are you (*sing.*)? _____

5. Who speaks German? _____

6. Who are you (*pl.*)? _____

7. Who am I? _____

8. Who is your friend? _____

Coordination of *Chi* as Subject

When the tense of the verb includes a *past participle*, the *auxiliary verb* will be in the *singular*.

When the auxiliary is **essere**, the past participle of the verb will be in the *feminine singular* when the person/group in question is composed of *females*; it will be in the *masculine* in all other cases.

Chi è and**ata** al mare? (*women*)	**Who** *went to the beach?*
Chi è **stato** in Cina? (*males and females*)	**Who** *has been to China?*
Chi si è vest**ita** in lungo?	**Who** *was wearing an evening gown?*
Chi si è **messo** l'impermeabile?	**Who** *wore a raincoat?*

When the auxiliary is **avere**, the *past participle* will be *in the masculine* (or coordinated with the direct object in *gender and number* when the object precedes the verb).

Chi ha dormito fino alle dieci?	*Who slept until ten?*
Chi ha comprato il pane?	*Who bought bread?*

---

esercizio   **8-2**

Translate the following sentences.

1. Chi viene alla festa? _____

2. Chi compra il pane? _____

3. Chi è quella ragazza? _____

4. Chi sono loro? _____

5. Chi acchiappa i topi? _____

6. Chi ha venduto il castello? _____

7. Chi l'ha venduto? _____

---

esercizio   **8-3**

Translate the following sentences. Use the present simple to translate the present progressive.

1. Who is leaving? _____

2. Who opened (*ha aperto*) the door? _____

3. Who must (*dovere*) pay the bill? _____

4. Who is selling the car? _____

5. Who wants dessert? _____

6. Who is going to the movies? _____

7. Who doesn't eat meat? _____

esercizio   8-4

Formulate the questions to which the following sentences are the answers.

1. L(o)'ha bevuto Enrico. _____

2. Giancarlo si è sbagliato. _____

3. Le hanno scelte i miei zii. _____

4. L(a)'ha vista mia madre. _____

5. Degli iscritti a Lettere, Ilaria si è laureata. _____

6. Li ho controllati io. _____

7. L(o)'ha rotto lei. _____

8. L(a)'ha rotta lui. _____

Chi as Direct Object

When **chi** is used as direct object, it translates the English *whom*. (In colloquial English, "who" is often used instead of "whom.")

Chi vedi?   *Whom do you see?*
Chi vedono?   *Whom do they see?*

esercizio   8-5

Translate the following sentences. Use the simple present.

1. Whom are you (*sing.*) calling? (*chiamare*) _____

2. Whom is she hiring? (*assumere*) _____

3. Whom does she love? _____

4. Whom are they contacting? _____

5. Whom do you (*pl.*) know? _____

6. Whom do we pay first (*per primi*)? _____

7. Whom must I call? _____

When **chi** is the direct object of a sentence and the tense of the verb includes a *past participle*, the auxiliary is **avere**, which will be coordinated with the *subject*, whereas the *past participle* will be in the *masculine singular*.

Chi ha licenzi**ato** tuo zio?	***Whom*** *did **your uncle** fire?*
Chi hanno premi**ato**?	***Whom*** *did **they** reward?*

Note: With the subject and the object of a sentence in the third person singular, as in «**Chi** ha licenziato **tuo zio**»? the sentence can mean: «**Chi** è la persona/le persone **che** tuo zio ha licenziato»? (***Whom*** *did **your uncle** fire?*) as well as, «**Da chi** è stato licenziato **tuo zio**»? (***Who*** *fired **your uncle**?*). Context will tell whether **chi** is used as subject or direct object.

esercizio	8-6

Translate the following sentences.

1. Chi avete visto allo stadio? _____

2. Chi vogliamo invitare? _____

3. Chi ha sposato tua sorella? _____

4. Chi hai chiamato per quel lavoro? _____

5. Chi hanno intervistato alla radio? _____

6. Chi ho assunto come consulente? _____

esercizio	8-7

Translate the following sentences. (Familiarity with the present perfect is necessary to do this exercise.)

1. Whom did you (*sing.*) call? (*chiamare*) _____

2. Whom did Nadia hire? (*assumere*) _____

3. Whom has she loved all her life? _____

4. Whom did they contact? _____

5. Whom did you (*pl.*) see? _____

6. Whom did you (*sing.*) meet? _____

7. Whom did we pay first? (*per primo*) _____

Di Chi? (Whose?)

English uses the determiner *whose* before nouns to inquire about *who is the owner of the thing owned.* Italian uses the *interrogative pronoun* **chi** accompanied by the preposition **di**.

Di chi è quella macchina?   ***Whose*** *car is that?*
Di chi è questo bambino?   ***Whose*** *baby is this?*

Translate the following sentences.

1. Whose suitcase is this? _____

2. Whose cats are those? _____

3. Whose flowers are these? _____

4. Whose car is that? _____

Whose can also be used in English to inquire about the relationship of possession between *a noun that is the predicate* of a sentence and *its unknown owner.* Italian uses **di chi**.

Di chi è **collega** (*predicate*) quel signore (*subject*)?   ***Whose colleague*** *is that gentleman?*
Di chi sono alleati (*predicate*) i ribelli (*subject*)?   ***Whose allies*** *are the rebels?*

esercizio   8-9

Translate the following sentences.

1. Di chi è sorella quella ragazza? _____

2. Di chi era fidanzato tuo cugino? _____

3. Di chi è figlio Giovanni? _____

4. Di chi sono fratelli Marcello e Piero? _____

5. Di chi sono amici quei ragazzi? _____

Whose can also precede a noun that is the *direct* or *indirect object* of a sentence.

Whose books *did you borrow?*

means

To whom *do the books you borrowed belong?*

For whose benefit did you make all those changes?

means

For the benefit of what person did you make all those changes?

In Italian we use the sentence «**di chi è (era/è stato**/etc.) **la cosa**... »? followed by a sentence introduced by the relative pronoun **che**.

Di chi sono **i libri che** hai preso in prestito?   ***Whose books*** *did you borrow?*
Di chi era **la casa che** hai comprato?   ***Whose house*** *did you buy?*

esercizio	8-10

Translate the following sentences.

1. Whose car is broken? (*rompersi*) _____

2. Whose cat got lost? (*perdersi*) _____

3. Whose CDs did you copy? _____

4. Whose wallet did the thief steal? _____

5. Whose motorbike are they riding? (*guidare*) _____

6. Whose painting are we buying? _____

7. Whose flowers are we picking? (*raccogliere*) _____

8. Whose packages are we shipping? _____

Chi Accompanied by Prepositions

Chi can be accompanied by other prepositions besides **di: a chi, con chi, per chi, da chi,** ecc., corresponding to the English *to whom, with whom, for whom, from/by whom,* etc. Preposition and pronoun are placed at the beginning of the clause they introduce.

A chi scrivi?   ***To whom*** *are you writing?*
Dimmi **a chi scrivi**.   *Tell me **to whom** you're writing.*
Con chi vai in campeggio?   ***With whom*** *are you going camping?*
Non so **con chi** andrò in vacanza.   *I don't know **with whom** I'm going camping.*

English often separates preposition and pronoun, but Italian does not. Therefore, a sentence such as:

Who(m) *are you buying that present **for**?*

can only be translated into Italian as:

Per chi stai comprando quel regalo?

esercizio   **8-11**

Translate the following sentences. Use the prepositions suggested in parentheses. Omit the subject. Use the simple present.

1. Who(m) does she live with? (*con*) _____

2. Who(m) do they work for? (*per*) _____

3. Who(m) are those flowers delivered by? (*da*) _____

4. Who(m) did he talk to? (*a*) _____

5. Who(m) are they buying a computer for? (*per*) _____

6. Who(m) do these shoes belong to? (*a*) _____

esercizio   **8-12**

Formulate questions to which the following sentences are the answers. When the answer you find listed in the exercise is in the first person singular or plural, you will need to formulate the corresponding question in the second person (and vice versa).

> EXAMPLE: **Answer**: Ho fatto X per Y. **Question**: Per chi hai fatto X?

1. Ha portato la cena alla sua vicina di casa. _____

2. Ho dedicato il libro a mio padre. _____

3. Andiamo in vacanza con i nostri amici. _____

4. *L'urlo* è stato dipinto da Munch. _____

5. Fa il prossimo film con Harrison Ford. _____

6. Puoi contare su di me. _____

7. Dovete consegnarlo a noi. _____

Che?/Cosa?/Che Cosa? (What?)

> **Che**?/**Cosa**?/**Che cosa**? is used to inquire only about *things*. It can be a *subject, direct object,* or *indirect object*. There is no set rule for choosing among **che**?, **cosa**?, or **che cosa**? although **che**? and **cosa**? are more colloquial.

> **Che cosa** succede?   *What's happening?*
> **Che** (**cosa**) hai fatto?   *What did you do?*

Di (che) cosa parlano?   ***What** are they talking **about**?*
Per (che) cosa ti sei battuto?   ***What** did you fight **over**?*

Che?/**Cosa?**/**Che cosa?** is invariable. As a *subject*, it takes the *third person singular*. The past participle will be *in the masculine*.

Che cosa è successo?   ***What** happened?*

 **esercizio**   **8-13**

Translate the following sentences. Use the simple present to translate the present progressive and the future.

1. What does she want? _____

2. What are they eating? _____

3. What is taking place in the square? (*succedere*) _____

4. What are you (*pl.*) thinking of doing? (*pensare di*) _____

5. What will we tell our parents? _____

6. What are you (*sing.*) buying? _____

esercizio   **8-14**

Translate the following sentences. Use the prepositions suggested in parentheses.

1. What are you (*sing.*) thinking about? (*a*) _____

2. What are they complaining about? (*lamentarsi di*) _____

3. What is she worried about? (*di*) _____

4. I don't know what to do. _____

5. Ask him what he wants to do. _____

6. I don't remember what I was saying. _____

Qual(e)? (What?) and Quali? (Which?)

Quale? is used for the *masculine and feminine singular*, and **quali?** for the *plural*. **Qual(e)** drops the **-e** before the third person singular of the verb **essere**, but it does not take an apostrophe: **qual è, qual era, qual è stata**.

Qual(e)/quali? is used:

- To inquire about the identity or quality of a *person* or *thing*.

Qual è il tuo cantante preferito?   ***Who*** *is your favorite singer?*
Qual è il loro numero di telefono?   ***What*** *is their telephone number?*

- To select one item out of a group that has been mentioned before.

Abbiamo molti **CD**. **Quale** vuoi?   *We have a lot of* ***CDs***. ***Which one*** *would you like?*
Vende dei bei vestiti, Signora.   *You sell beautiful dresses, Madam.*
        Quali sono della mia misura?   ***Which*** *(ones) are my size?*

---

esercizio   8-15

Add **quale** *or* **quali** *in the following sentences.*

1. Hai visto molte biciclette. _____ (*sing.*) hai comprato?

2. Dobbiamo scegliere un medico. _____ è meglio?

3. Ha buttato via molti vestiti. _____ (*pl.*) ha tenuto?

4. Puoi avere tre giocattoli. _____ vuoi?

5. Hanno fatto molte critiche al nostro progetto. _____ era la più seria?

6. _____ è il tuo cappotto?

7. _____ è il loro numero di telefono?

Che *and* Quale

Used as *pronouns*, **che** and **quale** are not interchangeable in Italian, as is the case with *what* and *which* in English. **Che cosa** means that the object we are inquiring about is indeterminate. **Quale** refers to a specific object.

Che cosa vuoi mangiare?   ***What*** *do you want to eat?*
Qual è il tuo colore preferito?   ***What*** *is your favorite color?*

---

esercizio   8-16

Complete the following sentences by adding **che/cosa/che cosa** *or* **quale/quali**.

1. _____ fai domani?

2. Ci sono molti libri. Vorrei sapere _____ (*sing.*) preferisci.

3. A _____ stanno giocando?

4. Dovete raccontare alla polizia _____ vi è successo.

5. Ha guardato molte riviste. A _____ (*sing.*) ha fatto abbonamento?

6. _____ le hai detto per farla piangere?

7. _____ dei suoi amici ti è più simpatico?

Quanto?/Quanta?/Quanti?/Quante? (*How Much?/How Many?*)

Quanto? means *how much/how many*. It can refer to *persons, animals,* and *things*. It can be used as *subject, direct object,* and *indirect object* accompanied by a preposition. It is coordinated in gender and number with the noun to which it refers. The default gender is masculine.

Quanti hanno firmato la petizione?	*How many signed the petition?*
Quante eravate?	*How many were you?*

Quanto fa? means that we purchased something and now we have to pay for it. It is mostly used in the singular.

«Eccole le sue arance, Signora».	*"Here are your oranges, Madam.*
«**Quanto fa**»?	*"How much are they?"*

Quanto costa? means that we are inquiring about a price. It becomes **Quanto costano?** when the thing we are inquiring about is in the plural.

«**Quanto costano** quelle scarpe»?	*"How much do those shoes cost?"*
«Cento euro».	*"One hundred euros."*

---

esercizio | 8-17

Complete the following sentences by adding **quanto/a/i/e**.

1. «_____ costa quella borsa»?

2. «Siamo andati tutti in barca». «_____ eravate»?

3. «Siamo andate tutte in barca». «_____ eravate»?

4. «Ho visto tantissimi uccelli, non so _____».

5. «Starò via alcuni giorni». «Sai dirmi esattamente _____»?

6. «Abbiamo invitato cento persone. Non so _____ accetteranno».

7. «_____ conta il suo appoggio»?

8. «A _____ ha venduto il dipinto»?

esercizio   8-18

Translate the following sentences.

1. "I'd like some bread." "How much?" _____

_____

2. "She bought (*ha comprato*) many books." "Do you know how many exactly?" _____

_____

3. "He buried (*ha sepolto*) five wives." "How many?!" _____

_____

4. "How much do those shoes cost?" _____

5. "How much do you (*sing.*) want for that boat?" _____

_____

6. "How much do those gloves cost?" _____

7. "How much is that dress?" _____

8. "Here is (*Ecco*) your cheese." "How much is it?" _____

_____

Quanto and *Ne*

When **quanto** is used to inquire *about a portion of a larger quantity*, it is accompanied by the partitive pronoun **ne**.

«Non c'è più pane».   *"There is no bread left."*
     «**Quanto ne** devo comprare»?   *"**How much** should I buy?"*
Voleva comprarsi un vestito.
     Non so dirti **quanti ne** ha provati!   *She wanted to buy a dress. I can't tell you **how**
                                           many she tried on!*

esercizio   8-19

*Translate the following sentences. Replace the nouns in parentheses with **ne**. Use the simple present.*

1. How many (*books*) are you (*pl.*) borrowing? (*prendere a prestito*) _____

_____

2. How much (*water*) do you (*sing.*) drink every day? _____

_____

3. How many (*friends*) is she inviting? _____

4. How much (*ice cream*) do you (*pl.*) want? _____

5. How much (*lettuce*) are you (*sing.*) buying? _____

6. How many (*letters*) are they sending? _____

esercizio   8-20

Translate the following sentences.

1. "He likes wine a lot." "How much does he drink?"

_____

2. "I'd like (*vorrei*) some oranges." "How many do you want, Sir?"

_____

3. "I'm buying ten computers." "How many are you buying?!"

_____

4. "He is learning another foreign language." "How many does he speak?"

_____

5. "How many rings does she wear?" "She wears eight."

_____

Unit 9

Relative Pronouns

A relative pronoun replaces an antecedent and introduces a dependent clause, called a *relative* or *adjective* clause. The phrase: ". . . which is now at MOMA," is meaningless unless it is preceded by a phrase that provides the antecedent: "The exhibit of Picasso's blue period, **which is now at MOMA**, is very interesting."

Italian has two sets of relative pronouns: invariable and variable.

Pronomi relativi (*Relative pronouns*)

INVARIABLE	VARIABLE	
che	il quale, la quale, i quali, le quali	who
che	il quale, la quale, i quali, le quali	whom
che	il quale, la quale, i quali, le quali	that
che	il quale, la quale, i quali, le quali	which
di cui/il cui	del quale, della quale, dei quali, delle quali	whose/ of which
cui/a cui	al quale, alla quale, ai quali, alle quali, per il quale, per la quale, per i quali, per le quali	for/to whom
da, con, ecc., cui	dal quale, dalla quale, dai quali, dalle quali, etc.	from, with, etc. whom/which

Italian relative pronouns can be used for *people, animals,* and *things.* In Italian you *cannot omit* a relative pronoun, as you may in English.

Ti è piaciuto il vino **che** abbiamo bevuto ieri sera?	*Did you like the wine (**that**) we drank last night?*
Il film **che** ha vinto il primo premio a Cannes è noioso.	*The film **that** was awarded the first prize at Cannes is boring.*
Il film, **che** è stato girato in Messico, è costato dieci milioni di euro.	*The film, **which** was shot in Mexico, cost 10,000,000 euros.*

The verb that follows a relative pronoun takes the *number* of *the antecedent to which the relative pronoun refers.*

Elena, che giocava a golf da anni,
  ha smesso improvvisamente.
Gli alpinisti che scaleranno
  l'Everest sono italiani.

Elena, who had been playing golf for years,
  suddenly stopped.
The mountain climbers who will climb
  Mount Everest are Italian.

If a *past participle* is used with the auxiliary verb **essere**, the past participle is *coordinated in gender with the antecedent*. If the auxiliary is **avere**, the past participle takes the masculine singular.

Parlerà con gli avvocati **che si sono
  occupati** della sua causa.
Le amiche che ho visto
  a cena sono spagnole.

She'll talk to the lawyers who
  took care of her lawsuit.
The girl friends (whom) I saw
  for dinner are from Spain.

Che (Who, Whom, That, Which)

Che can be used as *subject* and *direct object*. It cannot be accompanied by any preposition.

La bambina **che** (*subject*) suona
  il pianoforte è mia figlia.
La torta **che** (*direct object*) hai portato
  alla festa era buonissima.
La maestra lodò gli alunni **che** (*subject*)
  erano andati al museo (*masc. pl.*).

*The young girl **who** is playing the*
  piano is my daughter.
*The cake **that** you brought to*
  the party was excellent.
*The teacher praised the pupils **who***
  went to the museum.

---

esercizio   9-1

*Translate the following sentences. Use the pronoun **che**.*

1. The dog they got (*hanno preso*) never barks. _____

2. The boat she wants to buy is new. _____

3. The toys you left (*avete lasciato*) in the garden are all wet. _____

   _____

4. A wine we like a lot is *barbaresco*. _____

5. The architect who is designing (*progetta*) their new house is young. _____

   _____

---

esercizio   9-2

*Translate the following sentences. Use the pronoun **che**.*

1. Do you (*sing.*) know the scientist who will speak tonight?

   _____

2. The report Giulia is writing is very important.

_____

3. The apples that you (*pl.*) picked yesterday are very good.

_____

4. The earthquake that hit California was very strong.

_____

5. The young woman whom I met on vacation went to Australia.

_____

6. In 1908 Ford launched the Model T car, which cost $950.

_____

7. The workers she hired to build the house are Moroccans.

_____

Cui (to Whom, by Whom, Through Which, etc.)

Cui can only be used as *indirect object*. It is invariable and it can refer to people, animals, and things. **Cui** can be used without the preposition **a** when it means **al quale/alla quale, ai quali/alle quali**.

La persona **cui** devi consegnare questo pacco è al terzo piano.	*The person **to whom** you have to deliver this package is on the third floor.*
La ditta **cui** mi sono rivolto è molto affidabile.	*The firm **to which** I addressed my request is very reliable.*

esercizio	9-3

Translate the following sentences.

1. The problem you are referring to was solved.

_____

2. The person you (*sing.*) were thinking of (*pensare a*) for that job is not available.

_____

3. The friend Carla feels closest to is my sister.

_____

4. The cat they got so attached to (*affezionarsi a*) died suddenly.

_____

5. The lecture to which we went (*assistere a*) yesterday was interesting.

_____

6. The parish to which we belong will be closed (*verrà chiusa*).

_____

Verbs + *di*

Many verbs in Italian are followed by **di** (see the list in Appendix 2). Relative clauses introduced by **di cui** are therefore quite common.

Il problema **di cui** abbiamo parlato
   è stato risolto.

*The problem **about which** we talked
   was solved.*

 esercizio   9-4

*Translate the following sentences. Use **di cui**.*

1. At times I say things which I later (*poi*) regret (*pentirsi di*).

_____

2. This is the friend who(m) we talked to you about.

_____

3. He married a singer who you've heard of (*sentir parlare di*).

_____

4. The letter that they forgot was very important.

_____

5. We discussed the project for which I am responsible (*essere responsabile di*).

_____

6. On that shelf you will find the materials that you need.

_____

Cui can also be accompanied by other prepositions.

La casa **in cui** abito apparteneva ai
    miei nonni.
Gli arnesi **con cui** lavoro sono vecchi.

The house **in which** I live used to belong to
    my grandparents.
The tools **with which** I'm working are old.

esercizio   9-5

*Translate the following sentences. Use **cui** accompanied by the prepositions suggested in parentheses.*

1. The girl with whom I play tennis is an old friend. (*con*) _____

2. The boy who(m) she's talking with is my son. (*con*) _____

3. The candidate for whom I voted did not win the elections. (*per*) _____

4. The drawer in which you put your keys is empty. (*in*) _____

5. The desk on which you left your keys has been cleaned. (*su*) _____

6. The lady for whom he is buying a present is his wife. (*per*) _____

Variable and Invariable Relative Pronouns

Variable and invariable relative pronouns are interchangeable. Variable pronouns, which convey
gender and number, are used to avoid confusion about the antecedent to which we are linking
the relative clause. Variable pronouns can be used as *subject* and *object*, but they are mostly used
as *indirect objects* accompanied by *a preposition*. The variable pronoun is *coordinated in gender and
number with the antecedent* to which it refers.

La coda del pavone, **della quale** si
    vedeva solo la punta, era bellissima.
Molte favole mi ha raccontato la nonna,
    le quali erano divertenti e istruttive.

The peacock's **tail**, *of which you could only see
    the tip, was beautiful.*
My grandmother told me **many fables**,
    which were entertaining and instructive.

*Translate the following sentences. Use **il quale/ la quale, i quali/le quali** accompanied by the preposition suggested
in parentheses. (See Unit 13 on how to combine prepositions and definite articles.)*

1. The girl with whom I play tennis is an old friend. (*con*)

_____

2. The boy who(m) she's talking with is my son. (*con*)

_____

3. The candidate for whom I voted did not win the elections. (*per*)

_____

4. The drawer in which you put your keys is empty. (*in*)

_____

5. The desk on which you left your keys has been cleaned. (*su*)

_____

6. The parish to which we belong will be closed. (*a*)

_____

Il Cui/Di Cui/Del Quale (Whose)

English uses *whose* to convey possession. Italian uses:

- **cui** inserted between the article **il, lo, la, gli, le,** and *the thing owned.*

Il ministro le **cui** dichiarazioni sono state criticate ha dato le dimissioni.	*The minister **whose** statements were harshly criticized offered his resignation.*

- **del quale/della quale,** ecc., *placed after the object owned.* The variable form of the pronoun is coordinated with the *gender and number of the owner* to which it refers.

Un'attrice, **il cui nome** mi sfugge, raccoglie fondi per i malati di AIDS. Un'attrice, il nome **della quale** mi sfugge, raccoglie fondi per i malati di AIDS.	*An actress, **whose** name escapes me, launched an anti-AIDS campaign.*

esercizio   9-7

*Translate the following sentences. Use **cui**.*

1. Gianni, whose car was stolen, needs a taxi.

_____

2. The student, whose composition (*tema*) I read yesterday, writes well.

_____

3. The student, whose graduation (*promozione*) we are celebrating, is Maria's brother.

_____

4. Ada and Lia, whose intelligence you (*sing.*) appreciate, study medicine.

_____

5. He has written a book whose title I don't remember (*ricordare*).

_____

6. The scientist, whose discovery was in all the newspapers, died suddenly.

_____

7. The house, whose roof collapsed, was poorly (*male*) built.

_____

Double Relative Pronouns: *Chi, Quanto*

In Italian there are some relative pronouns that convey both a demonstrative (see Unit 10) and a relative pronoun. Therefore, they do not need an antecedent.

chi	those who
quanto	what/all that which
quanti, quante	all those who

Chi (*the One/Ones* **and** *Who/Whoever*)

Chi is a double pronoun that conveys the demonstrative pronoun **colui** and the relative pronoun **che/il quale**. **Chi** is invariable in gender and is followed by the verb in the third person singular, but it can refer to *a singular or a plural antecedent*. It can be used only for *people*.

Chi è passato di qui ha
   lasciato molte impronte.
Colui che è passato di qui ha
   lasciato molte impronte.

> *The person who came through here left a lot of prints.*

Chi lavora sodo viene premiato.   **Coloro che** lavorano sodo vengono premiati.
Those who work hard are rewarded.   *Whoever works hard is rewarded.*

esercizio   9-8

Translate the following sentences. Use **chi** *followed by a verb in the third person singular.*

1. Those who know me well trust me (*fidarsi di*).

_____

2. Those who pass the first test are admitted to the final (test).

_____

3. Those who gamble (*giocare d'azzardo*) often lose.

   _____

4. Those who need help must contact a physician.

   _____

5. Those who have read (*ha letto*) that book consider it a masterpiece.

   _____

Chi can combine *direct object* and *subject,* or *two direct objects.* English uses *who/whom.*

Ho scoperto **chi** ha rubato la sua collana.	→	Ho scoperto **colui** (*dir. object*) **che** (*subject*) ha rubato la sua collana.	*I discovered **who** stole her necklace.*
Ho riconosciuto **chi** hai salutato.	→	Ho riconosciuto **colui** (*dir. object*) **che** (*dir. object*) hai salutato.	*I recognized the person **who**(m) you greeted.*

Chi can also combine *indirect object* and *subject.*

Non faccio favori **a chi** non lo merita.	→	Non faccio favori **a coloro** (*indir. object, purpose*) **che** (*subject*) non lo meritano.	*I don't do favors **for those who** do not deserve it.*

esercizio   9-9

Translate the following sentences.

1. Tell me who(m) I have to send this package to. _____

2. I saw who(m) they invited. _____

3. Do you (*pl.*) want to know to whom they are selling their house? _____

   _____

4. We wish to thank those who helped us. _____

5. Don't trust (*fidarsi di*) those who make too many promises. _____

6. Whoever requests (*richiedere*) it will receive the brochure (*il depliant*). _____

   _____

7. She wants to know who earns (*guadagnare*) more than she. _____

   _____

Quanto (What, All That Which) and *Quanti/Quante (All Those Who)*

Used in the singular masculine, **quanto** means *what* and *all that which*. It can refer only to things. **Quanti/quante** means *(all) those who*. It can refer to both persons and things. It can be used as *subject*, *object*, and *indirect object* accompanied by a preposition.

Quanto dici è vero.	**What** *you say is true.*
Farò **quanto** mi è possibile.	*I'll do **all that** is in my power.*
Il rinfresco è riservato a **quanti** hanno ricevuto l'invito.	*The reception is reserved for (**all**) **those who** received an invitation.*

esercizio | 9-10

Translate the following sentences.

1. I'll remember (*ricordarsi di*) all that you (*sing.*) did for me.

   _____

2. She's addressing (*rivolgersi a*) all those who lost their money in that scam (*imbroglio*).

   _____

3. We're very sorry (*essere spiacente*) for what happened.

   _____

4. I will not add anything to what I said.

   _____

5. I'm giving you back all that I owe you.

   _____

6. What she's asking us is not much.

   _____

7. The judge ordered the arrest of all those who participated in the strike.

   _____

Dove (Where) and *Quando (When)* as Relative Pronouns

Dove and **quando** can introduce relative clauses, meaning: *the place in (at, to, etc.) which*, and *the time in which.*

È tornata al paese **dove** è nata.   *She went back to the country **where** she was born.*
Ti farò sapere **quando** potrai telefonargli.   *I'll let you know **when** you'll be able to call him.*

When **quando** is preceded by *a noun phrase specifying a moment in time* (*day, year, etc.*), colloquial Italian replaces it with **che**. English uses *when* or *that* or omits the pronoun altogether.

Non scorderò mai **il giorno quando**
    (**in cui**) ti ho incontrata.   *I will never forget **the day** (**when**)*
Non scorderò mai **il giorno che** ti   *I first met you.*
    ho incontrata.

but

Non scorderò mai **quando** ti vidi la   *I will never forget **when** I saw you the*
    prima volta.   *first time.*

cannot be turned into

Non scorderò mai **che** ti vidi la prima volta.

esercizio   **9-11**

Translate the following sentences.

1. Every time he gives a speech I fall asleep.

_____

2. The day (when) she will understand my troubles (*guai*) will be a great day.

_____

3. We took him to visit the village where his parents used to live (*erano vissuti*).

_____

4. Do you (*sing.*) know a store where I can find sandals?

_____

5. She will never forget (*dimenticare*) the year when her brother had that car accident.

_____

6. Elisa no longer knows where she put her car keys.

_____

7. The hotel where we spent so many nice vacations was closed.

_____

Demonstrative Pronouns

This/that are demonstrative pronouns referring to a noun or a sentence that precedes them. They can also refer to a person, or to present or past situations and experiences.

> *These sweaters look identical, but **this** (one) costs more than **that**.*
> ***This** is Elisabeth.*
> *Listen to **this**. You'll like it.*
> *I was thinking about **that**.*

The main demonstrative pronouns in Italian are **questo**, **quello**, and **ciò**.

Pronomi dimostrativi (*Demonstrative pronouns*)

questo/a, questi/e	this/these
quello/a, quelle/e	that/those
ciò	this/that

Questo (This) and Quello (That)

Questo and **quello** agree in gender and number with the antecedent they replace. They can refer to *people, animals*, and *things*. They can be used as *subject, object,* or *indirect object* accompanied by a preposition. **Questo** refers to an object/person *close to the speaker*, **quello** to an object/person *far away from both speaker and listener*.

> **Questo** è mio fratello.   ***This** is my brother.*
> **Quello** è mio fratello.   ***That** is my brother.*

| **esercizio** | **10-1** |

Translate the following sentences.

1. This is my book, that one is yours.

   _____

2. Take these shoes. Those are not your size. (*della tua misura*)

   _____

3. Those are your seats. (*il posto*)

   _____

4. This is our new math teacher (*fem.*).

   _____

5. Which dress do you prefer? This one or that one?

   _____

6. This is my wife.

   _____

7. Do you want these (*fem.*)?

   _____

8. My children? These are not my children.

   _____

Questo and **quello** can be reinforced with the adverbs of location **qui/qua** (*here*) or **lì/là** (*there*). **Qui/qua**, which point to a person/object close to the speaker, are used with **questo**. **Lì/là**, which point to a person/object far from the speaker, are used with **quello**. When used to refer to people, **questa qui**, **quella là**, ecc., carry a derogatory meaning.

Non ti fidare di **questa qui**.   *Don't trust **this one**.*
Non parlare a **quello là**.   *Don't talk to **that one**.*

esercizio	10-2

Translate the following sentences.

1. I don't want to talk about that (*woman*).

_____

2. Look (*sing.*) at that one, with that funny hat on his head!

_____

3. Listen (*sing.*) to this one, he thinks he knows everything.

_____

4. Are you buying this one (*masc.*)?

_____

5. We don't need these (*masc.*). They are useless.

_____

6. He is always thinking about those guys.

_____

7. With that one (*fem.*) you will not go far.

_____

Quello Verde, Quella Blu...

When the antecedent is accompanied by a qualifier, the demonstrative pronoun **quello** (rarely **questo**) can replace the noun and be followed by the qualifier, as English does with *the . . . one/ones.*

«**Quale sciarpa** vuoi»?
«**Quella blu**».
Ha scelto **quello di seta**.

"Which scarf do you want?"
"The blue one."
*She chose **the silk one**.*

esercizio   10-3

Translate the following sentences.

1. I like the long dress; she likes the short one.

   _____

2. Which one do you want? The yellow one or the red one? (*masc.*)

   _____

3. The big one is ideal for our family. (*fem.*)

   _____

4. Give me the black pen not the red one.

   _____

5. Put the large glass on the left and the small one on the right.

   _____

6. I like big dogs; she likes small ones.

   _____

Possessive Pronouns

In Italian, possessive pronouns are the same as possessive determiners (or adjectives). Unlike possessive determiners, pronouns *always* take the article.

Pronomi possessivi (*Possessive pronouns*)

il mio/la mia/i miei/le mie	mine
il tuo/la tua/i tuoi/le tue	yours
il suo/la sua/i suoi/le sue	his, hers, its
il nostro/la nostra/i nostri/le nostre	ours
il vostro/la vostra/i vostri/le vostre	yours
il loro/la loro/i loro/le loro	theirs

Possessive pronouns take the *gender* of the *thing owned* and the *person* of the *owner*.

La tua auto è nuova, **la mia** no.	*Your car is new, mine isn't.*
La vostra auto è nuova, **la nostra** no.	*Your car is new, ours isn't.*

When it comes to *number*, possessive pronouns agree in number with the object they refer to.

I tuoi vestiti sono nuovi, **i miei** no.	*Your clothes are new, mine aren't.*
I vostri vestiti sono nuovi, **i miei** no.	

Unlike in English, in the third person singular the possessive does not convey whether the owner is male or female.

> **La mia casa** è grande, **la sua** è piccola.

may mean

> *My house is large, hers is small.*

or

> *My house is large, his is small.*

Only context will help you understand whether the owner is male or female.

> La mia casa e quella di Giulia sono
> eguali, ma **la sua** ha un giardino
> più grande.

> *My house and Giulia's are the*
> *same size, but **hers** has a*
> *larger garden.*

In the third person plural, the possessive pronoun **loro** is the same for *both genders*; only the article tells whether the object owned is *feminine* or *masculine*, *singular* or *plural*.

> Abbiamo visto tanti progetti. Quello di **Anna e Giulia** è il migliore.

and

> Abbiamo visto tanti progetti. Quello di **Luca e Massimo** è il migliore.

become

> Abbiamo visto **tanti progetti.**
>   **Il loro** è il migliore.
> Abbiamo guardato **molte fotografie.**
>   **Le loro** sono le più interessanti.

> *We have seen many projects.*
>   ***Theirs** is the best.*
> *We looked at many photographs.*
>   ***Theirs** are the most interesting.*

esercizio   11-1

Translate the following sentences.

1. These shoes are not yours, they are mine. _____

2. The pink house is theirs. _____

3. My cat is affectionate, theirs is not. _____

4. Her house is as big as yours (*pl.*). _____

5. My pen? No, this is yours (*sing.*). _____

6. My camera is here; hers is on the shelf. _____

7. Your (*sing.*) skis are ready, his aren't. _____

esercizio   11-2

Translate the following sentences.

1. Il tuo libro ha avuto molto successo, il suo (*di Angela*) no.

2. Abbiamo venduto la nostra barca. Adesso usiamo la sua (*di Enrico*).

_____

3. Il cappello blu non è il tuo. È il suo. (*di Pietro*)

_____

4. Prendi i guanti gialli, quelli rossi sono i suoi. (*di Elena*)

_____

5. «Hanno visto le vostre figlie alla festa»? «No, ma hanno visto le sue». (*di Giovanni*)

_____

Possessive pronouns can be used as *subject*, *object*, or *indirect object* accompanied by a preposition.

Dei due progetti, **il tuo** (*subject*) è il migliore.	*Of the two projects, **yours** is the better.*
Ho letto i vostri due progetti e preferisco **il suo** (*direct object*).	*I read your projects, and I prefer **his**.*
Le ho parlato delle mie vacanze, non **delle vostre** (*indirect object*).	*I talked to her about my vacations, not **about yours**.*

esercizio	11-3

Translate the following sentences.

1. Her house is smaller than mine. _____

2. I don't like his proposal, but I like yours (*sing*). _____

3. You're (*sing.*) always thinking about (*pensare a*) his problems, never about mine! _____

_____

4. Our interests conflict (*contrastare con*) with theirs. _____

5. Here (*Ecco*) are your coats. Take yours (*sing.*). _____

6. Are they taking care of (*occuparsi di*) my taxes or hers? _____

_____

7. Don't buy their house; buy his. _____

8. We invested in his fund, not in yours (*pl.*). _____

A Friend of Mine, of Yours, etc.

When we wish to select one item out of a group, as we do when we say: "He is a friend of mine," Italian uses the following construction.

È uno **dei miei amici**.   *He is one **of my friends**.*

but

È un amico **dei miei**.

means

*He is a friend **of my parents**.*

esercizio   11-4

Translate the following sentences.

1. That policeman is a friend of ours. _____

2. She is talking to a teacher of his. (*parlare con*) _____

3. A cat of theirs got lost. (*perdersi*) _____

4. Two colleagues of hers speak Chinese. _____

5. Can we borrow (*prendere*) a car of yours (*sing.*)? _____

6. A daughter of mine lives in Australia. _____

7. I work with a cousin of yours (*pl.*). _____

Mio (My) and Il Mio (Mine)

In Italian, possessive pronouns always carry the article. They convey the idea that an object belongs to A rather than to B *or* that the owner possesses a specific object in a group of like objects.

«Ci sono tante sciarpe.   *"There are so many scarves here.*
  Qual è **la tua**»?   *Which one is **yours**?"*
«**La mia** è quella rossa».   *"**Mine** is the red one."*

But the sentence «Quella casa è **mia**» means «That is **my** house/That house **belongs to me**." Only context will tell you whether to use **mio** or **il mio**.

esercizio | **11-5**

Translate the following sentences. Use the possessive pronouns.

1. Her computer is faster than mine. _____

_____

2. That bike is hers, not this one. _____

_____

3. Your (*sing.*) job is as interesting as his. _____

_____

4. Which skirt is mine? The blue one. _____

_____

5. Don't take (*sing.*) that raincoat. It's hers. _____

_____

6. Our plan is better than yours (*pl.*). _____

_____

7. This is our address. Do you want theirs too? _____

_____

Indefinite Pronouns

Indefinite pronouns suggest an indefinite quantity or number, or a person/thing whose precise identity is irrelevant or not known.

Ho visto molte case.	*I saw a lot of houses.*
Alcune erano belle,	***Some** were beautiful*
ma troppo care.	*but too expensive.*
Non ne ho parlato con	*I didn't talk about it with*
nessuno.	***anyone.***

Here follows a list of the most important indefinite pronouns.

alcuni, alcune/qualcuno	some/any/a few
altro	else
un altro, un'altra/gli altri, le altre	another/(the) others
chiunque	anyone/anybody
ciascuno, ciascuna/ognuno, ognuna	each/everyone
gli uni... gli altri/le une... le altre	some . . . the others
l'un l'altro, l'un l'altra	each other/one another
molti, molte	many/a lot
molto, molta	much
nessuno	no one/nobody
niente/nulla	nothing
parecchi, parecchie	a lot/several
pochi, poche	a little/too little/few
poco, poca	a little/too little
qualcosa	something/anything
qualcuno	someone/somebody
tanti, tante	so much, so many
tanto... quanto, tanta... quanta	as/so much . . . as
tanti... quanti, tante... quante	as many . . . as
troppo, troppa	too much
troppi, troppe	too many
tutti e due, tutte e due	both
tutti, tutte	(all) everyone
tutto, tutta	everything
uno, una	one

Indefinite pronouns can be used as *subject*, *direct object*, and *indirect object* accompanied by a preposition.

Qualcuno (*subj.*) vuole parlarti.	***Someone*** *wishes to talk to you.*
Volete mangiare **qualcosa** (*dir. obj.*)?	*Do you want **something** to eat?*
Non dirlo **a nessuno** (*indir. obj.*).	*Don't say it **to anyone**!*

Double Negatives

English does not use double negatives, whereas Italian does.

Non vedo **nessuno**.	**Non** ha comprato **nessun vestito**.
*I **don't** see **anyone**.*	*She **didn't** buy **any** dress.*
*I see **no one**.*	*She bought **no dress**.*

When **nessuno** or **niente** are at the beginning of the sentence, however, the negative particle **non** is dropped.

Nessuno la vuole assumere.

or   *No one wants to hire her.*

Non la vuole assumere **nessuno**.

[*Not:* **Nessuno non** la vuole assumere.]

Gender and Number

The default gender of indefinite pronouns is masculine, as usual. However, when we know that the indefinite pronoun refers to a female person or group, most pronouns will take *the feminine*.

È venuta **una** a cercarti.	**Ciascuna** di voi prenda un tutù.
Someone *came looking for you.*	*Take a tutu **each**, please.*

Most pronouns also vary *in number*.

Ho parlato con **molti** di loro.	Ha visto **alcune** di voi alla festa.
*I spoke with **many** of them.*	*She saw **some** of you at the party.*

esercizio   12-1

Translate the following sentences.

1. Nessuno vuole il pesce. _____

2. Ognuno può pensare quello che vuole. _____

3. Sono andati tutti e due a sciare. _____

4. Ciascuno è contento di quello che ha. _____

5. Tutti sono contenti. _____

6. Qualcuno ti cerca. _____

7. La porta era aperta. Chiunque può aver rubato la radio. _____

_____

8. Franca non ha visto nessuno. _____

9. «Vuoi delle arance»? «Ne voglio qualcuna». _____

10. Non si parlano più l'uno con l'altro. _____

11. Questa gonna non mi piace. Posso provarne un'altra? _____

_____

---

esercizio　　**12-2**

Translate the following sentences. Use the simple present to translate the present progressive.

1. Is someone coming? _____

2. No one is going with them. _____

3. I'm inviting both to the party. _____

4. There is someone on the phone for you. _____

5. Anyone could (*saprebbe*) write that novel. _____

Uno: *One* and *Someone*

Italian uses the indefinite pronoun **uno** in many instances when English uses *someone*.

> È venuta **una** a cercarti.　　　　Ho incontrato **uno** che ti conosce.
> *Someone came looking for you.*　　*I met **someone** who knows you.*

Alcuno (*Some*), Qualcuno (*Any*), and Nessuno (*None*)

Italian uses **alcuni** mostly in the plural, meaning *some*. When the sentence is negative, we use **nessuno,** which is only singular.

> «Hai visto che belle mele»?　　　　*"Did you see those beautiful apples?"*
> 　　«Ne ho mangiate **alcune**».　　　　　*"I ate **some**."*

but

> «Hai visto che belle mele»?　　　　*"Did you see those beautiful apples?"*
> 　　«Non ne ho mangiata **nessuna**».　　　*"I didn't eat **any**."*

English uses *some* in interrogative sentences when the answer is expected to be positive; it uses *any* when the answer is expected to be negative.

«Guarda che belle mele!	*"These apples look great!*
Ne vuoi **qualcuna**»?	*Do you want some?"*
«Sì, grazie».	*"Yes, please."*
«Hai mangiato le mele a pranzo.	*"You had apples at lunch.*
Ne vuoi **qualcuna per cena**»?	*Do you want any dinner?"*
«No, grazie».	*"No, thank you."*

When we know that the answer is negative, the question will be in the negative as well.

«**Non** hai visto **nessun** film»?	*"Didn't you see any film?"*
«**No, non** ne ho visto **nessuno**».	*"No, I didn't see any."*

We use **alcuni, alcune,** and **qualcuno, qualcuna** interchangeably. **Qualcuno** does not take the plural.

«Guarda che belle mele»!	*"These apples look great!"*
«Ne ho assaggiata **qualcuna**,	*"I tried some, but they*
ma non erano buone».	*didn't taste good."*

Chiunque (*Anyone* and *Whoever*)

The indefinite Italian pronoun **chiunque** translates the English indefinite pronoun *anyone* and the relative pronoun *whoever*.

Chiunque vorrebbe tre mesi	*Anyone would like three months'*
di vacanza all'anno.	*vacation a year.*
Chiunque te l'abbia detto, ti ha mentito.	*Whoever told you that lied to you.*

Tutti (*Everyone* and *All*)

Italian uses **tutti** in many instances when English uses *everyone*.

Sono andati via **tutti**.	Non puoi accontentare **tutti**.
Everyone has left.	*You cannot make everyone happy.*

Ciascuno (*Each*) and Ognuno (*Everyone*)

Ciascuno and **ognuno** are used to indicate a group of people or things, considered in their single components. They are used only in the singular.

Ha parlato con **ciascuno** di loro.	**Ognuno** è libero di fare quello che vuole.
She spoke to each of them.	*Everyone is free to do what they like.*

Tutti e due (*Both*)

Tutti e due is used in Italian in situations where English uses *both (of)*, but in a negative clause we can only use **nessuno dei due**, followed by the verb in the singular.

«Dove sono Pietro e Vittorio»?	*"Where are Pietro and Vittorio?"*
«Sono andati **tutti e due** alla partita»./	*"**Both of them** went to the game."/*
«**Nessuno dei due** è andato alla partita».	*"**Neither of them** went to the game."*

esercizio | **12-3**

Translate the following sentences. Use the simple present to translate the present progressive and the simple future.

1. I'm inviting all my friends, but only some will come. _____

   _____

2. No one is ready for the trip. _____

3. Are you (*sing.*) talking to someone? _____

4. Will you remember (*ricordarsi di*) everyone? _____

5. Anyone would want (*vorrebbe*) that house. _____

6. Is everyone ready? _____

7. "Aren't you (*sing.*) inviting anyone?" "No, I am not." _____

8. Neither of the two want to answer your (*sing.*) question. _____

   _____

9. Both are answering my questions well. _____

Molti (Many) and Tanti (So Many)

Molti and **tanti** convey the notion of great quantities or numbers, but **tanti** conveys the idea of excessive or greater than expected quantity.

Ne ha comprati **tanti** (libri)!	*He bought so many (books)!*

When **molti, parecchi, pochi,** and **tanti** are used to refer to people, but the group of which they represent a part is left implicit, Italian can use the construction: **Erano in molti/parecchi/ pochi/tanti a...** + *noun or verb in the infinitive.*

Sono **in tanti** a volere la guerra.	***So many** want to go to war.*
Erano **in molti** alla partita di calcio.	*There were **lots** (of people) at the soccer game.*

esercizio 12-4

Translate the following sentences.

1. Many are coming (*pres. simple*) to my party. _____

2. Several came (*sono venuti*) to greet my uncle. _____

3. Many would like to marry her. _____

4. So many would like to marry her. _____

Indefinite Pronouns + *Ne*

Indefinite pronouns are often used to indicate a part out of a larger whole.

Alcuni dei miei amici non verranno al matrimonio.	***Some of my friends*** *will not come to the wedding.*

Indefinite pronouns can therefore be accompanied by the pronoun **ne**.

I miei amici? **Ne** verranno solo **alcuni** al matrimonio.	*My friends? Only **some** will come to the wedding.*
«Hai mangiato le arance»?	*"Did you eat any oranges?"*
«**Ne** ho mangiata **una**».	*"I ate **one**."*

esercizio 12-5

*Translate the following sentences. Use **ne** when the indefinite pronoun refers to a part of a larger whole.*

1. She looked for an excuse for her behavior but couldn't find any. _____

_____

2. They didn't find anyone. _____

3. Everyone has the right to express their opinion. _____

4. "Do you (*sing.*) want some peaches?" "Give me only a few." _____

_____

5. "We have a lot of figs. Do you (*sing.*) want any?" "No, thanks." _____

_____

6. There was no one around (*in giro*). _____

7. Everyone was shocked when they heard the news. _____

_____

_____

Indefinite Pronouns + *Di* (*Among*)

Several indefinite pronouns can be followed by **di** (and **in**) or **tra** + *noun, pronoun,* ecc. The pronoun may be in the singular or the plural. The preposition may be followed by a *noun,* an *adjective,* or a *pronoun.*

Hai visto **qualcosa di interessante** (*adj.*) alla mostra?	*Did you see **anything interesting** at the exhibit?*
[*Not:* Hai visto **qualcosa interessante** alla mostra?]	
Solo alcuni di voi (*pron.*) la capiscono.	*Only some of you understand her.*
Mi piace **tutto di lei** (*pron.*).	*I like everything about her.*
C'è **qualcosa in lui** (*pron.*) che non capisco.	*There is something in him I don't understand.*
Niente di ciò che (*rel. pron.*) dici potrà farmi cambiare opinione.	*Nothing of what you say will make me change my mind.*
Non riesce a finire **nessuno dei suoi progetti** (*noun*).	*She cannot complete any of her projects.*

esercizio	12-6

Translate the following sentences.

1. Molti di voi si sono dimenticati di firmare. _____

2. Non c'è niente di importante in quel messaggio. _____

_____

3. Parecchi dei miei amici non parlano l'inglese. _____

4. Niente di ciò che dici ha senso. _____

5. Umberto non ha mai fatto niente di buono nella vita. _____

_____

6. Qualcosa in lei non mi convince. _____

7. Mi piace tutto di lei. _____

8. Molto di quanto avete fatto è stato inutile. _____

esercizio	12-7

Translate the following sentences.

1. One of you stole (*ha rubato*) the painting. _____

2. Each of the candidates (*fem.*) passed the exam. _____

3. Some of us agree with you (*sing.*). _____

4. The director spoke with each one of us. _____

5. She doesn't talk to any of them. _____

Indefinite Pronouns That Refer Only to Things

Some indefinite pronouns refer only to things or to an abstract quantity.

Capisce anche **troppo** per la sua età.   *She understands way **too much**, given her age.*

molto, molta	much
niente/nulla	nothing
poco, poca	a little/too little
qualcosa	something/anything
tanto... quanto, tanta... quanta	as much . . . as
troppo, troppa	too much
tutto, tutta	everything

Tutto (*Everything*)

When used in the masculine singular, **tutto** means *everything*.

Tutto è in ordine.   ***Everything** is in order.*

esercizio	12-8

Translate the following sentences.

1. They don't want anything. _____

2. She wants something from me. _____

3. Nothing works (*funzionare*) here. _____

4. You (*pl.*) never eat anything. _____

5. She eats nothing. _____

6. Everything went well. _____

7. Don't do anything else. _____

esercizio	12-9

Translate the following sentences.

1. Hai preparato tutto? _____

2. Non ha visto niente. _____

3. Cercano qualcosa da regalarle. _____

4. «È tardi, ma vuoi qualcosa da mangiare»? «No, grazie». _____

_____

5. «Devi avere fame! Vuoi qualcosa da mangiare»? «Sì, grazie». _____

_____

6. Non abbiamo trovato niente di bello in quel negozio. _____

_____

7. Dice qualcosa di nuovo? _____

8. Desidera altro, Signora? _____

9. Non posso fare nient'altro per lui. _____

Tanto... (So/As Much...) and Quanto (So/As)

Tanto and **quanto** are used to introduce comparisons.

Il gelato piace **a lei tanto quanto a lui**.　　*She likes ice cream **as much as he** does.*

Poco (Too Little) and (a Little)

In Italian, **poco** means *very little* or *not enough*. When we wish to convey *a little* we use the indefinite phrase **un po' di**.

Ho **poco** pane.　　*I have **very little/not enough** bread.*
Ho **un po' di** pane.　　*I have **a little/some** bread.*

Translate the following sentences.

1. Don't give me so much wine. I only want a little. _____

_____

2. "Does he drink a lot of wine?" "No, he drinks very little." _____

_____

3. Do you want a little cognac? _____

_____

4. Aren't you eating (*simple pres.*) too much? _____

_____

5. "Do we have enough cheese for the party?" "We have even (*anche*) too much." _____

_____

PART II

PREPOSITIONS

Prepositions are invariable words that link the components of a sentence. Each preposition can play different functions: *I'm at home*, or *He's at ease*. Conversely, different prepositions have similar uses: *in the morning, at dawn*. In other cases, it is the verb, noun, or adjective that determines the preposition to be used: *You're **responsible for** your deeds. We'll **arrive at** London Heathrow*.

These general principles hold for Italian as well. However, in several instances the preposition used in one language is different from the one used in the other. For example, both Italian and English use **di** (*of*) to qualify or specify characteristics of things and persons: **Parlo della tua amica** (*I'm speaking of your friend*). But Italian uses **a** in the expression **Penso a lui**, while English uses *of*: *I'm thinking of him*.

Keeping in mind, therefore, that general rules do not always hold true, we can say that, in Italian, prepositions perform the following functions.

They precede a noun or pronoun, forming an *indirect object* (**complemento indiretto**), also called *prepositional phrase*.

Vado in **chiesa con Maria**.	*I'm going **to church with Maria**.*
Vado in **chiesa con lei**.	*I'm going **to church with her**.*

They introduce a *verb in the infinitive*. In English, the verb will be in the gerund (unless the verb is in the infinitive, which includes the preposition *to*).

Penso **di** cambiare lavoro.	*I'm thinking of changing jobs.*
Incomincia **a nevicare**.	*It's starting to snow.*

Some prepositions and adverbs used as prepositions *can be followed by a conjunction that introduces a dependent clause.*

L'ha fatto **prima che potessi** avvertirlo.	*He did it **before I could** warn him.*
L'ho visto **dopo che** ti ha parlato.	*I saw him **after** he talked to you.*

Some prepositions can be used as *adverbs.*

Vado **su**.	*I'm going **upstairs**.*

Prepositions can also accompany the verb and modify its meaning, rather than introduce the word that follows. English is rich in such *phrasal verbs: to break down, put off, work out, give up*, etc. Although less common, they exist in Italian, too. **Tirare**, for example, means *to pull, but* **tirare su** can mean *to build something (quickly); to lift someone's spirits; to raise children.*

Ha **tirato su** la baita in tre giorni.	*He **put together** the cabin in three days.*
Quella bella notizia mi ha **tirato su**.	*That nice news **lifted my spirits**.*
Irene **tira su** bene **i suoi figli**.	*Irene is **raising her children** well.*

The Most Commonly Used Prepositions

The following are the most important Italian prepositions, listed here from the most commonly used to the least commonly used.

Preposizioni (*Prepositions*)

di	of
a	at/to
da	from/by
in	in (into)
su	on (onto)
con	with
per	for
tra/fra	between/among

When used by themselves, they are called **preposizioni semplici** (*simple prepositions*). Linked to the definite articles **il, lo/l', la/l', i, gli, le**, they form the **preposizioni articolate**. In order to ease pronunciation, Italian will:

- Double the **-l** between the preposition and the articles that start with **l**:

     a + la spiaggia   →   alla spiaggia.

- Turn the **-i** in **di** into **-e**: **di + lo**   →   dello.

- Turn **in** into **ne**: **in + il**   →   nel; in + le   →   nelle.

Con gives the option of using the **preposizione articolata**—especially the forms **col** and **coi**—or of using the *preposition* and the *article* separately.

Vado al mare **colla** zia.   }   *I'm going to the beach with*
Vado al mare **con la** zia.   }   *my aunt.*

The following table shows the forms taken by the preposition when combined with the article.

Preposizioni articolate

	IL	LO/L'	LA/L'	I	GLI	LE
di	del	dello/dell'	della/dell'	dei	degli	delle
a	al	allo/all'	alla/all'	ai	agli	alle
da	dal	dallo/dall'	dalla/dall'	dai	dagli	dalle
in	nel	nello/nell'	nella/nell'	nei	negli	nelle
su	sul	sullo/sull'	sulla/sull'	sui	sugli	sulle
con	col	collo/coll'	colla/coll'	coi	cogli	colle

Tra/fra do not form **preposizioni articolate**. **Tra** and **fra** have the same meaning. We prefer using the one that avoids alliteration with the words that follow.

tra fratelli	*rather than*	**fra fratelli**	*between/among* brothers
fra due treni	*rather than*	**tra due treni**	*between* two trains

esercizio   13-1

In the following sentences, combine the simple preposition and the article in parentheses to form the corresponding **preposizione articolata**.

1. Non tirare la coda _____ gatto. (*a + il*)

2. Ho messo la biancheria _____ lavatrice. (*in + la*)

3. Appendiamo il quadro _____ studio. (*in + lo*)

4. _____ colle c'era la neve. (*Su + il*)

5. Dove sono i giocattoli _____ bambini? (*di + i*)

6. Andranno _____ sua festa domani sera. (*a + la*)

7. L'esplorazione _____ spazio incominciò _____ anni cinquanta _____ XX secolo. (*di + lo*), (*in + gli*), (*di + il*)

8. _____ finestra si vede il mare. (*Da + la*)

9. Ha piantato delle viti _____ collina. (*su+ la*)

10. Hai parlato _____ dottore? (*con + il*)

11. Non ha ereditato niente _____ suoi genitori. (*da + i*)

12. Le chiavi non sono _____ cassetto. (*ne + il*)

13. Hai parlato _____ zii delle vacanze? (*a + gli*)

14. _____ scavi hanno trovato una tomba ricchissima. (*In + gli*)

15. La luce _____ stelle è fortissima in cima _____ monti. (*di + le*), (*a + i*)

16. Non ha messo la data _____ assegni. (*su + gli*)

17. Avete cercato _____ tasche? (*in + le*)

18. _____ *Appennini* _____ *Ande* è un romanzo per ragazzi. (*Da + gli*), (*a + le*)

19. Non aspettatevi molto _____ negoziato. (*da + il*)

20. Abbiamo riflettuto a lungo _____ sue parole. (*su + le*)

21. _____ hotel non c'era nessuno. (*A + lo [l']*)

22. Guarda tutti _____ alto in basso. (*da + lo [l']*)

23. Non ci piace la torta _____ arancia. (*a + la [l']*)

24. C'era la disperazione _____ suoi occhi. (*in + i*)

25. Il motore a scoppio fu inventato _____ Ottocento. (*in + lo [l']*)

26. Hai bisogno _____ macchina? (*di + la*)

27. Usa ancora i libri scolastici _____ anno scorso. (*di + lo [l']*)

28. Non è amato molto _____ sue sorelle. (*da + le*)

29. Non fidarti _____ estranei. (*de + gli*)

30. Non ricordo il titolo _____ libro. (*di + il*)

31. _____ sforzo che hai fatto, meriti un premio. (*Con + lo*)

32. I soldati uscirono _____ scoperto. (*a + lo*)

33. _____ miei tempi si andava a piedi. (*A + i*)

34. Ho messo la picozza _____ zaino. (*su + lo*)

35. Hanno messo tante luci _____ tetti delle case! (*su + i*)

36. Ha fatto quella foto _____ obiettivo (*lense*) sbagliato. (*con + lo [l']*)

37. _____ orizzonte si vedeva una sottile linea rossa. (*Su + lo [l']*)

38. Il coniglio venne catturato _____ aquila. (*da + la [l']*)

39. La serratura _____ armadio è rotta. (*di + la*)

40. _____ fortuna che ho, perderò il treno. (*Con + la*)

41. Hanno parlato _____ guardiani del magazzino. (*con + i*)

42. Era stremata _____ sforzo. (*da + lo*)

43. Sono _____ acqua alla gola. (*con + la* [l'])

44. Abbiamo messo dei fiori freschi _____ altare. (*su + lo* [l'])

45. L'aereo finì _____ occhio del ciclone. (*in + lo* [l'])

46. Non parla più _____ zii. (*con + gli*)

47. Giochi ancora _____ tue cugine? (*con + le*)

Other Parts of Speech That Function as Prepositions

Other words besides the **preposizioni semplici** can function as prepositions. Some must be followed by a **preposizione semplice** (listed without parentheses below). Some can stand alone; others can stand alone or be followed by a preposition.

Parts of speech that function as prepositions

ADVERBS

accanto (a)	close to, by
attraverso (di)	across from, through
contro (di)	against
davanti (a)	before, in front of
dentro (a)	inside
dietro (a/di)	behind
dopo (di)	after
insieme a, con	together with
invece di	instead of
fuori (di)	outside of, without
prima (di)	before
sopra (a)	over, above
sotto (a)	below, beneath

ADJECTIVES

lontano (da)	away, far from
lungo	alongside
secondo	according to/in someone's opinion
vicino (a)	near, close to

NOUNS

riguardo a	regarding, concerning
rispetto a	in comparison to, with

PRESENT AND PAST PARTICIPLES

durante	during
eccetto	except (for)
escluso	excluding
mediante	through
nonostante	despite
paragonato a	compared to/with

CONJUNCTION

senza (di)	without

What Is a Preposition?

Several words play the function of prepositions but are not prepositions to begin with. *Words that do not link two elements of a sentence are not prepositions.* Compare the following sentences.

È partita **dopo Natale**. (*prepos.*)	She left **after Christmas**.
Dovevi dirmelo **prima**. (*adverb*)	You should have told me **sooner**.
Camminiamo **lungo la riva**. (*prepos.*)	Let's walk **alongside the bank**.
Quel film è **lungo**. (*adj.*)	That movie is **long**.
Corre dietro alle donne. (*phrasal verb*)	He's a womanizer.
L'hanno **fatto fuori**. (*phrasal verb*)	They **did** him **in**.

esercizio | 13-2

Translate the following sentences.

1. Il cavallo è dentro il recinto. _____

2. Si è nascosta dietro la casa. _____

3. L'aereo vola sopra la valle. _____

4. Molti insetti vivono sotto terra. _____

5. Passiamo da voi dopo cena. _____

6. Eccetto Massimo, siamo tutti d'accordo. _____

7. Annibale entrò in Italia attraverso il Passo del Piccolo Gran San Bernardo.

   _____

8. Secondo me, ha ragione lui. _____

9. Nonostante i nostri avvertimenti, sono partiti per l'Amazzonia.

_____

10. Siete tutti contro Paola? _____

11. Durante la Quaresima non mangiano carne. _____

_____

Prepositional Locutions

Some adverbs, adjectives, nouns, etc., can be combined with the **preposizioni semplici** to form *prepositional locutions*.

Prepositional locutions

a favore di	in favor of
a fianco di	on the side of (met.)/by
a forza di	by dint of
a meno di	without
a vantaggio/svantaggio di	to the advantage/disadvantage of
a/per causa di	because of
al fine di	in order to
al posto di	in the place of
all'esterno di	without/outside
all'interno di	within/inside
allo scopo di	with the aim to
da parte di	on the part of
graziea	thanks to
in base a/sulla base di	on the basis of
in cambio di	in exchange for
in cima a	on top of
in confronto a	in comparison to/with
in mezzo a	in the middle of
per colpa di	due to/by fault of
per conto di	on behalf of
per il bene di	for the sake of
per mezzo di	by means of

esercizio   13-3

Translate the following sentences, choosing among the prepositional locutions listed above.

1. L'ho fatto per il bene di mia sorella.

_____

2. Gianni non può vivere senza di lei.

_____

3. Grazie a voi, abbiamo ottenuto il prestito.

_____

4. Mario ha ottenuto il lavoro, invece di Michele.

_____

5. A causa degli errori dell'avvocato abbiamo perso la causa.

_____

6. Prima di noi in questa valle non era venuto nessuno.

_____

7. Mia madre è triste perchè viviamo tutti lontano da lei.

_____

8. Posso sedermi vicino at te?

_____

9. Insieme a lui andrei in cima all'Everest.

_____

Prepositions and Subordinate Clauses

Prepositions can also be used to introduce a _verb_, thus introducing a _subordinate or dependent clause_, so called because the sentence is meaningless if the main clause is left out: ... **di andare**... (_to go_ . . .) does not tell us by itself what we are talking about.

Ho deciso **di andare** a casa.   _I decided **to go** home._

Several prepositions can be used this way: **di, a, da, per** (and **senza**). Other prepositional locutions can also introduce a verb. _The verb is in the present or past infinitive._ English can use a preposition followed by the infinitive or the gerund; it can use a dependent clause introduced by a conjunction or a completely different syntactical construction.

Ci ha detto **di aspettare**.   _He told us **to wait**._
Ho una fame **da morire**.   _I'm dying **of hunger**._

In Italian we can use the *verb + preposition + infinitive* construction only in two cases:

- When the subject of the dependent clause is the same as *the subject of the independent clause.*

  Ho voglia di andare al cinema.   ***I want to*** go to the movies.

- When the subject of the dependent clause is *the direct or indirect object of the independent clause.*

  Vi prego **di fare silenzio.**   →   Prego **voi** (*dir. obj.*)   *I'm asking **you***
                                              di fare silenzio.   ***to keep quiet.***

  Le ho chiesto **di telefonare.** →   Ho chiesto **a lei** (*ind. obj.*) *I asked **her to call**.*
                                              di telefonare.

esercizio   13-4

Translate the following sentences.

1. Vado a sciare domenica. _____

2. Vai a casa di Maria a studiare? _____

3. Dille di non comprare il latte. _____

4. Hanno cercato di avvisarli. _____

5. Vanno all'aeroporto a prenderla. _____

6. Abbiamo bisogno di aiuto per finire questo lavoro. _____

   _____

7. Dammi un libro da leggere. _____

8. Lo sgridarono per aver fatto chiasso. _____

Classification of Prepositions

Italian calls **complementi** (*complements*) the prepositional phrases made of *a preposition + a noun or pronoun.* We need complements because subject and verb often do not carry sufficient information: "I want" is incomplete if we don't convey *what* we want.

Italian grammar books can explain prepositions and complements in two ways.

They list **le preposizioni** (especially the simple ones, **di**, **a**, **da**, ecc.) and all the possible **complementi** that each preposition can introduce. Under **di**, for example, you will find listed the **complemento di specificazione** (*specification*): **l'albero dell'ulivo** (*the olive tree*); the **complemento partitivo** (*partitive*): **molti di noi** (*many of us*); the **complemento di denominazione** (*denomination*): **la città di Firenze** (*the city of Florence*); **complemento di origine** (*origin*): **sono di Roma** (*I am from Rome*); ecc.

Alternatively, grammar books list all the **complementi** and explain what prepositions can be used to convey them. For example, **il complemento di stato in luogo** (*place where*), a prepositional phrase that conveys that a person or thing *is* in a certain place, can be introduced by several prepositions: **in**, **su**, **da**, **tra**, **sopra**, **sotto**, ecc.

Siamo **in casa**.	*We're **at home**.*
Il libro è **sul divano**.	*The book is **on the sofa**.*
Il gatto è **sotto il letto**.	*The cat is **under the bed**.*
Il cane è **dietro la casa**.	*The dog is **behind the house**.*

The use of the prepositions and their classifications in Italian is not easy to grasp. We will take an approach that we hope will make it easier for the student to learn the prepositions and how to use them. In the following chapters we cover:

- Specification/possession

- Place

- Time

- Purpose, company, and agency

- Means, qualities, and causes

With this approach, one preposition can be used to form different **complementi**. The preposition **a**, for example, will be listed in sections on *place, time, manner, means*, etc., conveying:

Place where	Sono **a casa**.	*I'm **at home**.*
Specific point in time	Pranzo **a mezzogiorno**.	*I have lunch **at noon**.*
Manner	È fatto **a mano**.	*It is **handmade**.*
Means	Ci è andato **a piedi**.	*He went there **on foot**.*

Appendix 2 reports most **complementi** and the prepositions used to introduce them.

Possession and Specification

Phrases such as "my mother's cat," "a marble statue," "the fear of war," "a ten-month-old baby," convey the idea that *something/someone belongs to someone or something else*, or they add *information about a person or object*: what material something is made of, what the object of our emotions is, how old something is, and so on.

To convey *possession* and *specification* (the complement that adds information about someone or something), Italian mostly uses the preposition **di** (and at times **con**, as English does with *with*). English conveys these ideas by using:

- *Noun + noun*, in which the first noun modifies or describes the second.

l'albero dell'ulivo	*the olive tree*
gli **impiegati del Comune**	*City Hall staff*

- *Noun + 's + noun*, in which the noun that is modified takes the possessive form.

il cane **di Nicola**	*Nicola's dog*
il giornale **di oggi**	*today's newspaper*

- *Noun + preposition + noun/name.*

le pagine **del** libro	*the pages of the book*
il timore **della** guerra	*the fear of war*

esercizio 14-1

Translate the following phrases, using the noun + noun, or the noun + 's + noun structure.

1. il gatto di Maria _____

2. la coda del gatto _____

3. il giornale della settimana scorsa _____

4. l'albero di pesco _____

5. i funzionari delle Nazioni Unite _____

6. un ragazzo di quindici anni _____

7. un libro di trecento pagine _____

8. il tavolo di legno _____

esercizio   14-2

Translate the following sentences, following the pattern of the phrases in Italian listed under esercizio 14–1.

1. He's writing a two-volume book. _____

2. She has a ten-year-old girl. _____

3. She doesn't want a marble table. _____

4. We cannot find Maria's dog. _____

5. They evacuated (*hanno evacuato*) all U.N. officials. _____

_____

6. The cat's tail is black and white. _____

7. Are you reading last month's newspapers? _____

8. We want to plant five apple trees. _____

esercizio   14-3

Translate the following sentences.

1. Vuoi vedere il giornale di ieri? _____

2. Dobbiamo scrivere un saggio di trenta pagine. _____

_____

3. Voglio mettere una moquette di lana. _____

4. La partenza del gruppo è fissata per le nove di mattina. _____

_____

5. Scrive libri di francese. _____

6. Quell'armadio (*closet*) è pieno di vestiti vecchi. _____

_____

7. Il cane di Giulia è morto. _____

su (on), circa (about), riguardo (concerning)

Other prepositions can be used to convey specific information about a person, animal, or thing.

su	on, about
circa	about, regarding
con l'eccezione di	with the exception of
in relazione a	in connection with
riguardo (a)	concerning, regarding

Sta scrivendo un libro **sulla**
   prima guerra mondiale.
Per informazioni **riguardo a quella**
   pratica, rivolgetevi al capufficio.

*She's writing a book **on***
   World War I.
*For information **regarding that***
   ***file**, ask the office manager.*

esercizio 14-4

Translate the following sentences.

1. They are inquiring (*indagare*) about her role in the firm's financial crisis.

_____

2. I don't have news about your mother's illness, Mr. Pertini.

_____

3. Will she make that movie on the French Revolution?

_____

4. I know nothing concerning your request, Sir.

_____

5. We all left (*partire*), with the exception of Antonella.

_____

6. Mario hasn't told me anything else about that deal.

_____

7. He writes books on Russian literature.

_____

di (of), tra/fra (between/among)

Di and **tra/fra** are used to indicate the whole out of which we select a part. English uses *of* or *between/among*.

Molti di noi non andranno a votare.   *Many of us will not vote.*
Era seduta **tra** Maria e Elsa.   *She was seated **between** Maria and Elsa.*
Tra tutti i vestiti che ha provato   *There was only one red dress*
ce n'era solo uno rosso.   ***among all those she tried on.***

esercizio	14-5

*Translate the following sentences. Use **di** to translate* of *and **tra/fra** to translate* between/among.

1. Some of the students protested (*hanno protestato*).

_____

2. There are criminals among his friends.

_____

3. She's the smartest of them all.

_____

4. Some members of the team refuse (*rifiutarsi*) to play.

_____

5. A few of you will vote (*voteranno*) for the new candidate.

_____

6. Is there a physician among the passengers?

_____

del, dello, della, dei, degli, delle: Specification and Partitive Article

As seen in Unit 6, **del, dello, della**, ecc., can be used as a *partitive article*.

Dammi **dell**'acqua.   *Give me **some** water.*
Compri del pane?   *Will you buy **bread**?*

The partitive article, **del, della,** ecc., can be accompanied by other prepositions, *except* **di**.

Viene **con degli** amici.   *She's coming **with some** friends.*
Ho scritto **a dei** giornalisti.   *I wrote **to some** journalists.*

When **del, delle,** ecc., is used as a partitive article that would require the preposition **di** in its place we use the *indefinite determiners* **alcuni, qualche,** ecc.

Parlo **di alcune persone** che ho visto   *I'm talking **about some people** I saw at*
al cinema.   *the movies.*

esercizio	14-6

*Translate the following sentences. Use **del, della,** ecc., meaning* some, a few, *etc., unless the preposition preceding it is **di**. Use the prepositions suggested in parentheses.*

1. I'm going to the mountains with some expert guides. (*con*)

   _____

2. Did you (*pl.*) get in touch with lawyers? (*con*)

   _____

3. I was talking about some acquaintances I met at the theater. (*di*)

   _____

4. She saw a documentary on some strange fish. (*su*)

   _____

5. I thought of (*pensare a*) some solutions to your (*sing.*) problem.

   _____

6. We went through (*passare per*) some wild valleys.

   _____

7. They forgot (*dimenticarsi di*) some appointments.

_____

8. I bought these presents for some cousins (*fem.*) of mine. (*per*)

_____

Italian uses the **di** + *noun* construction to convey measurement.

Abbiamo fatto un viaggio **di tre ore**.	*We made a **three hours' journey**.*
Porta un vestito **di taglia 42**.	*She wears a **size 42 dress**.*

But to convey capacity, Italian uses **da** + *unit of measurement or size*.

Hai comprato una bottiglia **da cinque litri**?	*Did you buy **a five-liter bottle**?*
Regalava ai passanti banconote **da 500 euro**.	*He was giving away **five hundred euro banknotes** to passersby.*

Specification Without *di* (*of*)

In the language of publicity, journalism, and bureaucracy, Italian sometimes omits the preposition **di** between two nouns, but, unlike English, it does not invert the word order.

lo scalo delle merci	→	**lo scalo merci**	*the delivery dock*

There is no set rule to help you decide in what cases the preposition **di** can be dropped. In journalism especially, it is a matter of style. Here follow some examples.

il controllo passaporti	passport control
il giornale radio	radio news program
il luna park	amusement park
il parco giochi	playground
la rivendita sali e tabacchi	drugstore/tobacco store
la scuola guida	driving school

Verbs + *di*

As remarked, prepositions can introduce an entire sentence. **Di** is often used when English uses the verb in the infinitive. Here follow the most common verb forms that take **di** (see also Appendix 2), followed by a noun or a verb in the infinitive.

avere bisogno di qualcuno, qualcosa/di fare	to need
avere fretta di fare	to be in a hurry
avere paura di qualcuno, qualcosa/di fare	to be afraid of
avere voglia di qualcosa/di fare	to wish, desire, crave
decidere di fare	to decide
dimenticarsi di qualcuno, qualcosa/di fare	to forget
essere capace di fare	to be able, to be capable of

fidarsi di qualcuno	to trust someone
finire di fare	to finish doing
importare di qualcosa a qualcuno	for someone/something to matter to someone; to care about someone
parlare di qualcuno, qualcosa/di fare	to talk about
pensare di fare	to think of
prendersi cura di qualcuno	to look after
pretendere di	to pretend; to claim
ricordarsi di qualcuno, qualcosa/di fare	to remember
sapere di qualcosa	to taste
smettere di fare	to stop doing
sperare di fare	to hope to do
trattarsi di	to be a matter for/of
vestirsi di (rosso, blu, ecc.)	to be dressed in (red, blue, etc.)

esercizio   14-7

Translate the following sentences.

1. Spero di rivederli presto. _____

2. Pensavamo di fare un salto da Maria. _____

3. Elena ha deciso di emigrare in Australia. _____

4. Ti sei dimenticato di chiudere il garage un'altra volta! _____

_____

5. Non ho nessuna intenzione di seguire i suoi consigli. _____

_____

6. A Riccardo non importa niente di noi. _____

7. La nonna si è presa cura di lei dopo la morte dei suoi genitori. _____

_____

8. Non vi fidate di noi? _____

9. Non hanno più bisogno di vendere le azioni. _____

10. Giancarlo non ha voglia di fare i compiti. _____

11. Pensiamo di aprire un negozio. _____

Place

"Place" is used here to refer to literal and metaphorical situations conveying the *place where* something happens, or *moving toward, from, through,* etc., *a place, a person, or a situation.*

Vado **a scuola**.	*I'm going **to school**.*
Sono **in ufficio**.	*I'm **at the office**.*
Sono **di Roma**.	*I'm **from Rome**.*
Emma ha divorziato **da Renato**.	*Emma got divorced **from Renato**.*

English is rather strict in the use of prepositions of place. If you are *moving toward something* you have to use the preposition *to* or one of its compounds: *into, onto, toward,* etc. If you are *moving away from something,* you have to use the preposition *from.* Italian is much more flexible in the use of prepositions, as the table below shows.

Prepositions Indicating Place

place where	**di, a, da, in, su, per, tra**
motion toward	**di, a, da, in, su, per, tra**
motion from	**di, da**
motion through	**di, da, in, per, tra**
distance	**a**
separation	**da**
origin	**di, da**

In Italian, prepositions of place *do not tell us whether the action regards movement or not,* as English prepositions of place often do. Other words in the sentence, especially the verb, convey this information. Compare the following:

Sono a scuola dalle otto all'una.	*They are **in** school from 8 A.M. to 1 P.M.*
Vanno a scuola a piedi.	*They **walk to** school.*

In Italian, the preposition is used to express other aspects of one's position is space. For example, we use **a** when we talk about being in a position *at* a point (**a casa**) and we use **in** when we place something *within* a larger area (**in Italia**).

Abito **in Via Mazzini**.	*I live **in Via Mazzini**.*
Abito **in Via Mazzini al numero 25**.	*I live **at 25, Via Mazzini**.*

We can say:

Esco **di** casa, *or* Esco **da** casa,	*I'm walking **out of** the house. /*
or Esco **dalla** casa (**da + la**)	*I'm leaving the house.*
[*Not*: Esco **della** casa. (**di + la**)]	

In, a, da, and *su* are the most widely used prepositions to indicate *place where* or *motion toward*. They can be used by themselves or with articles to form the **preposizioni articolate**.

a and in

As stated, **a** is used to speak of *place as a point*, and **in** is used to locate something *within a larger area or a three-dimensional space.*

Abitano **a** Pechino.	*They live **in** Beijing.*
Vanno **a** Mosca.	*They're going **to** Moscow.*
Viviamo **in** Inghilterra.	*We live **in** England.*
Si trasferisce **in** Germania.	*She is moving **to** Germany.*

With nouns in the singular, **a** and **in** are mostly used without an article. In particular, the article is omitted before names (Naples, China, etc.), but it is used when:

- The name of a country or a region is in the plural: **gli Stati Uniti** (*the United States*), **le Prealpi** (*the Pre-Alps*).

    Stanno per emigrare **negli Stati Uniti**.   *They are about to emigrate **to the United States**.*

- Regions and other geographical areas carry the article as part of their name: **il Sahara, il Kent, la Loira, il Salento**, etc.

    Nella Loira ci sono molti castelli.   *There are a lot of castles **in the Loire Valley**.*

---

esercizio   15-1

*In the following sentences, insert either **a, al, alle**, ecc., or **in, nello, negli**, ecc., as appropriate.*

1. Gli uccelli migrano _____ sud in autunno.

2. Hanno una bella casa _____ Prealpi venete.

3. Hanno fatto il trasloco _____ Parigi.

4. Si è fatto una casetta _____ montagna.

5. Non le piace vivere _____ città.

6. Ha vissuto _____ paesi più strani.

7. Voliamo _____ Praga domani.

8. Facciamo un viaggio _____ Cina.

9. Hanno passato due mesi _____ Cina meridionale.

10. _____ nord c'è la stella polare.

11. Passeranno il Natale _____ India.

12. Hanno comprato una villetta _____ periferia.

---

esercizio | **15-2**

Translate the following sentences.

1. I'm flying (*simple pres.*) to London tomorrow. _____

2. They go into the countryside every weekend. _____

3. They spend every summer (*tutte le estati*) at the sea. _____

4. They live in town, whereas (*invece*) we live in the country. _____

   _____

5. You (*sing.*) cannot drive (*andare in macchina*) to St. Peter's. _____

   _____

6. Shall we meet (*vedersi*) in Vienna? _____

7. He is moving to New Mexico. _____

8. I'm moving downtown. _____

9. Do you (*pl.*) like life out there in the country (*provincia*)? _____

   _____

Islands

With the names of islands, it is at times difficult to decide whether to use **in** or **a**. Size is usually a determinant. We say **in Sicilia** (*in Sicily*), but **a Cuba** (*in/on Cuba*), and **all'isola d'Elba/all'Elba** (*on the island of Elba*), **all'isola di Pasqua** (*on Easter Island*), **all'isola di Man** (*on the Isle of Man*), etc.

Here follow the names of some islands that take either **in** or **a**:

in   Corsica, Groenlandia (*Greenland*), Inghilterra (*England*), Sicilia (*Sicily*),
             Nuova Guinea (*New Guinea*)
a   Capri, Cipro (*Cyprus*), Martha's Vineyard, Long Island, Cuba
alle   Bahama (*The Bahamas*), Baleari (*The Balearic Islands*), Eolie, Seychelles, Maldive

in (*in*) and *su* (*on*)

Italian uses *in* or *su* + *article* (*preposizione articolata*) + *noun* to convey *place where* or *motion toward* when referring to *an enclosed physical place, a surface,* or *a vehicle.*

In is used with buildings or other settings that *enclose* space.

Quelli che hanno perso la casa   *Those who lost their homes*
   nel terremoto sono **nella chiesa**.   *in the earthquake are **in the church.***
Siamo entrati **nello stadio**   *We walked **into the stadium** through*
   dalla porta sbagliata.   *the wrong door.*

esercizio   15-3

Translate the following sentences.

1. I bambini sono andati nello studio di papà. _____

2. Non mettere le scarpe sul divano! _____

3. Le due squadre sono entrate nello stadio. _____

4. Siamo sul campo di calcio, pronti a giocare. _____

5. Non sono saliti tutti sull'autobus. _____

6. Il cardinale ha celebrato i funerali di stato nella cattedrale. _____

   _____

7. Sulla vetta c'eravamo solo noi. _____

8. Guarda quante vele ci sono sul mare oggi! _____

Su is used with *means of transportation* and with *areas* or *surfaces,* as English does with *on.* But we say **al pianterreno/al terzo, quinto, piano,** ecc., (*on the ground floor/on the third, fifth floor,* etc.). (The **pianterreno** corresponds to the first floor in the United States, **il primo piano** to the second floor, and so on.)

Ho lasciato la borsa **sul tavolo**.   *I left my purse **on the table.***
Salì **sul palcoscenico** e si mise a cantare. *He got **onto the stage** and started to sing.*
Non sono mai stata **sulla luna**.   *I have never been **on the moon.***
Salite **sull'autobus**!   *Get **on the bus**!*

esercizio	15-4

Translate the following sentences.

1. You left (*hai lasciato*) the pot on the stove (*gas*). _____

2. In that room there are only two beds. _____

3. May I put my sweaters in that closet (*armadio*)? _____

4. It's time to get back (*risalire*) on the bus. _____

5. In the pot there are only six potatoes. _____

6. Do you have any money (*dei soldi*) in your wallet? _____

7. The two teams are entering the stadium. _____

8. Is there room (*posto*) for eight on the boat? _____

su (on), sopra (over/above), and sotto (under/below)

In Italian, **su** means *on*; **sopra** means *over/above*. **Su** and **sopra** can often be used interchangeably.

L'aeroplano vola **sulla città**. /	*The airplane flies **over the city**.*
L'aeroplano vola **sopra la città**.	
Il libro è **sulla tavola**. /	*The book is **on the table**.*
Il libro è **sopra la tavola**.	

Italian contrasts **sopra**, meaning *above/upstairs*, with **sotto**, meaning *under/below/downstairs*.

Il libro è **sopra il tavolo**.	*The book is **on the table**.*
Il gatto è **sotto il tavolo**.	*The cat is **under the table**.*
Abitano **sopra di noi**.	*They live **one floor up/above us**.*
Abitano **sotto di noi**.	*They live **one floor down/below us**.*
[*Not*: Abitano **su di noi**.]	

esercizio	15-5

*Insert su, sopra, or sotto in the following sentences. Form **preposizioni articolate** when possible.*

1. Il cappello è _____ la sua testa.

2. Jules Verne è l'autore di *Ventimila leghe* _____ i mari.

3. Il lampadario è appeso _____ il tavolo.

4. Ha messo una lampada alogena _____ la scrivania.

5. La gatta si è nascosta _____ il letto.

6. Sono stati _____ il Monte Everest.

7. Non le piace andare _____ la acqua.

8. Viviamo all'ultimo piano. Non vogliamo avere nessuno _____ di noi.

Place and Function: *in, da, a*

When talking about a place, we may refer to the building or site as a *physical place*, or to *the function or activity* that happens there. This distinction is apparent in the English words *house*, which refers to a building, and *home*, which carries emotional overtones. *Prepositions of place* may be used to convey the difference between the two usages. Compare the following:

I bambini sono **in chiesa**.	*The children are **at/in church**.*
Quelli che hanno perso la casa nel terremoto sono **nella chiesa**.	*Those who lost their homes in the earthquake are **in the church**.*

The fact that the children are *at/in church* tells us that they are attending a religious service, which occurs in a building that we call *the church*. But when we say that the people are hosted *in the church*, we mean that they are physically in that building. At times, of course, we may mean both at once.

È **in chiesa**.	*He's **at church**. / He's **in the church**.*

In general, when we refer mostly to *function*, Italian has two options:

- **in** + *noun* (*without the article*): **in chiesa**, **in ospedale**, **in drogheria**, ecc.

Ha dovuto andare **in ospedale**.	*He had to go **to the hospital**.*

- **da** + *article* (**preposizione articolata**) + *noun* when *place* is conveyed through the profession, service, or just the social relation occurring there: **dal macellaio**, **dal dottore**, **dal barbiere**, **dalla zia**, ecc.

Siete stati **dal professore**?	*Did you go talk **to your professor**?*

When we use **a** + *article* (**preposizione articolata**) + *noun*: **all'università**, **allo stadio**, **alla stazione**, ecc., we may refer to *physical place and/or function*.

Sono andati **al cinema**.	means	*They went **to see a movie**.*
		*They went **to the movie theater**.*
Lavora **all'università**.		*She's a **university professor**.*

As usual, all prepositions can convey *place where* or *motion toward*.

Sono **dal medico**.	*I'm **at the doctor's** (office).*
È andata **dal pediatra**?	*Did she go **to the pediatrician**?*
Vado io **in latteria**.	*I'm going **to the store** (dairy).*
Siete a cena **dalla zia**?	*Are you **at your aunt's** for dinner?*

Common Expressions of Place That Use **in** (*in/[at]/to*) Without the Article

ACTIVITIES/INSTITUTIONS

(la) banca	bank
(la) biblioteca	library
(la) casa	home (*also* **a casa**)
(la) chiesa/parrocchia	church/parish
(la) classe	classroom
(la) clinica	clinic
(il) collegio	boarding school
(il) giardino	garden/backyard
(l') ospedale	hospital
(lo) studio (for professionals)	office/at work
(il) teatro	theater (also *a teatro*)
(il) tribunale	court
(l') ufficio (for employees)	office/at work
(l') università	university/on campus
(but) **a (la) scuola**	school

SHOPPING

(la) birreria	brewery
(la) calzoleria	shoe repairer
(la) cartoleria	stationery store
(la) farmacia	pharmacy/drugstore
(la) latteria	milk and cheese store
(la) libreria	bookstore
(la) macelleria	butcher shop
(la) merceria	haberdashery
(la) pizzeria	pizza place
(la) profumeria	perfume store/drugstore
(la) rosticceria	deli
(la) tabaccheria	cigarette store/drugstore
(la) tintoria	cleaners

SPORTS, LEISURE, AND TRAVEL

(il) campeggio	(to go) camping/camping site
(l')hotel/(l')albergo/(il) motel	hotel/motel
(la) palestra	gym
(la) pensione	family-run hotel
(la) piscina	swimming pool
(la) stazione	bus/railway station

| **esercizio** | **15-6** |

Translate the following sentences.

1. Siamo stati in casa tutto il fine settimana. _____

2. Elisabetta non va piú in chiesa da quando aveva quindici anni. _____

_____

3. «Dov'è Pietro»? «È andato in panetteria». _____

4. Lo trova in ufficio, Signor Cellini. _____

5. Suor Chiara è in parrocchia. _____

6. Devo proprio andare in banca. Non ho più un soldo. _____

_____

7. Quanto tempo sei stata in ospedale? _____

8. Passano tutta l'estate in giardino. _____

9. Ho tenuto mio figlio a casa stamattina. Aveva la febbre. _____

_____

10. Venite a teatro con noi domani sera? _____

11. È incredibile: mia figlia si diverte a scuola. _____

12. Ci incontriamo in piazza? _____

| **esercizio** | **15-7** |

*Add **in** or **a** in the following sentences.*

1. Luisa è andata _____ teatro con sua madre.

2. Non voglio andare _____ ospedale!

3. Ha passato il sabato pomeriggio _____ chiesa a pulire i banchi.

4. Mia figlia è andata _____ banca da sola per la prima volta.

5. Lo sai che non puoi portare i criceti _____ scuola.

6. Stia attento, sa, che la trascino _____ tribunale!

7. È una settimana che sono chiusa _____ casa con l'influenza.

8. L'avvocato non è _____ studio, oggi.

9. Ai bambini fa bene andare _____ piscina.

10. Preferisci stare _____ hotel o _____ campeggio?

11. _____ cartoleria adesso vendono anche i giornali.

The preposition **da** is used to indicate place and movement toward, as in **da me** (*at my place*), **da te** (*at your place*), etc. Other examples of **da** used with relationships are:

da mia madre	(at/to) my mother's place
dai miei	(at/to) my parents' place
dai miei amici	(at/to) my friends' place
dalla sua amante	(at/to) his lover's place
dalla zia	(at) my aunt's

Dallo, **dalla**, ecc., is also used with providers of services, as in **dal barbiere** (*at/ to the barber's*). A list of providers of services follows:

Terms That Take **dallo**, **dalla**, ecc.
_____

PROVIDERS OF SERVICES

dall' avvocato	lawyer's office
dal barbiere	barber
dai casalinghi	houseware store
dal calzolaio	shoe repairer
dai Carabinieri	at the Carabinieri (*a police corps*)
dal commercialista	CPA
dal dentista	dentist's office
dall' estetista	beauty parlor
dal ferramenta	hardware store
dal fioraio	florist
dal fruttivendolo	greengrocer/ vegetable store
dal gelataio	ice-cream parlor
dal giudice	judge/in court
dall' infermiera (*more rarely,* **dall'infermiere**)	nurse's office
dal lattaio	milk and cheese store
dal macellaio	butcher
dal medico, dottore (*and all specializations*)	physician, doctor's office/clinic
dalla merciaia	fabric and sewing store (haberdashery)
dal notaio	solicitor who takes care of administrative matters
dal panettiere	baker, bakery
dalla pettinatrice/dal parrucchiere	hairdresser
dal salumiere	deli
dal tabaccaio	tobacco store/drugstore

esercizio   15-8

*Insert **da**, **dal**, **dallo**, ecc., in the following sentences.*

1. L'ho visto _____ tabaccaio.

2. Passiamo la domenica pomeriggio _____ me o _____ te?

3. Non si può più andare _____ quel lattaio. Non ha mai il latte fresco.

4. Sono passata _____ infermiera a fare il vaccino antiinfluenzale.

5. Il prezzo della carne è salito alle stelle _____ nostro macellaio.

6. Mia sorella ha portato sua figlia Nicoletta _____ pediatra.

7. Non va più _____ barbiere perché ha deciso di lasciarsi crescere i capelli.

8. Sono _____ notaio per la lettura del testamento.

Other nouns commonly take **al** to mean *at/in/to*.

Terms That Take **al**, **allo**, ecc.

GENERAL ACTIVITIES

all'asilo	nursery school/kindergarten
al centro commerciale	shopping mall
al doposcuola	after-school activities
al negozio	store
all'ospedale	hospital
alla Polizia	Police
al Pronto Soccorso	emergency room
allo stadio	stadium
al supermercato/al supermarket	supermarket
al tribunale	courthouse
all'ufficio postale/alla posta	post office
all'università	college/university

EATING

al bar	bar
al caffè	café
al ristorante	restaurant
al self service	self-service
alla tavola calda	fast-food place

SPORTS AND LEISURE

al cinema	movie theater
al circolo di bocce	bocce club
al club	club
al conservatorio	conservatory/school of music

| al luna park | amusement park |
| al parco giochi | playground |

TRAVELING

all'aeroporto	airport
al controllo passaporti	passport control
alla dogana	customs
all'hotel/all'albergo/al motel	hotel/motel
alla stazione (dei treni, degli autobus, dei taxi)	train, bus, taxi station
al terminal	terminal
all'uscita/alla porta d'imbarco	gate

esercizio 15-9

Translate the following sentences.

1. Portiamo i bambini al parco giochi? _____

2. Non è a casa. È all'università. _____

3. Passano il sabato pomeriggio al centro commerciale. _____

_____

4. I signori passeggeri sono pregati di presentarsi all'uscita numero otto. _____

_____

5. C'era una lunga fila al controllo passaporti. _____

6. A mezzogiorno mangiamo sempre alla tavola calda. _____

_____

7. C'è qualcosa di interessante al cinema? _____

esercizio 15-10

*Insert **al, allo, alla**, ecc., in the folllowing sentences.*

1. Venite anche voi _____ stadio?

2. Non arriveremo mai _____ aeroporto con questo traffico!

3. Per fortuna, l'ambulanza è arrivata _____ ospedale in tempo.

4. Dobbiamo essere _____ terminal alle sei di mattina.

5. _____ stazione dei taxi non c'era neanche una macchina!

6. Lasciate i bambini tutti il pomeriggio _____ doposcuola?

7. I dimostranti si erano piazzati _____ ingresso della sala dei congressi.

| **esercizio** | **15-11** |

*Insert **a/al, in/nel, da/dal, su*** in the following sentences.

1. Ho prenotato una visita _____ medico.

2. Si sono visti _____ casa di mia cugina.

3. Si sono visti _____ mia cugina.

4. Ha passato la notte _____ biblioteca a studiare per l'esame.

5. Non le piace vivere _____ decimo piano. Soffre di acrofobia.

6. _____ luna non c'è acqua.

7. Mangiano almeno una volta la settimana _____ pizzeria.

8. Quanti passeggeri c'erano _____ nave che è affondata?

9. Andiamo _____ avvocato per parlare del divorzio.

10. Ci vediamo _____ bar alle due?

11. Il cane non è stato fermo un momento _____ veterinario.

12. I bambini si sono nascosti _____ camera da letto.

13. Non mette mai la macchina _____ garage.

14. Ha piantato tre peri _____ giardino.

15. Si è chiusa _____ casa tre mesi fa e non ne è più uscita.

Note: We use **al**, **allo**, ecc., for the body and its parts:

Si è fatta male **alla gamba**.   Porta tre anelli **alla mano sinistra**.
*He hurt **his leg**.*   *She wears three rings **on her left hand**.*

da and di (from, out of, and off)

We use **da** to convey *motion from, origin, distance, and motion out of a container.* But we use **di** with the verb **essere** to mean *being born into a family, a group, or a place.*

Sono partiti **da New York** tre ore fa. *They **left New York** three hours ago.*
Vengono **da Milano**. *They are coming from Milan.*
Siamo a dieci chilometri **da Parigi**. *We are ten kilometers **away from Paris**.*
Lo ha tolto **dalla borsa**. *He took it **out of the bag**.*

but

Sono **di Milano**. *They are from Milan.*
È **di buona famiglia**. *She comes from a good family.*

esercizio	15-12

*Translate the following sentences. Use **da** and **di**.*

1. La nostra vicina di casa passa tutto il giorno a guardare dalla finestra. _____

_____

2. Hai tirato giù quel brutto quadro dal muro? _____

3. Suo (*masc.*) padre era di famiglia benestante. _____

4. Devo togliermi un sassolino dalla scarpa. _____

5. Ha visto che si è tolta la fede dal dito? _____

6. Togliti quelle idee pazze dalla testa! _____

7. Vivono a due isolati da noi. _____

8. Stai lontano dal cancello. Quel cane è pericoloso. _____

9. Tenete le mani lontante dalle porte. _____

esercizio	15-13

*Insert **da** (**dal**, ecc.) or **di**.*

1. Partiamo _____ aeroporto della Malpensa.

2. Non siamo più molto lontani _____ vetta.

3. Sei _____ origine scozzese?

4. La polizia cercò di fare allontanare gli ostaggi _____ finestra.

5. Avete preso un numero per la lotteria _____ sacchetto?

6. Il mago estrasse la carta giusta _____ mazzo.

7. Si sono trasferiti a duecento metri _____ loro genitori.

8. Il suo fidanzato è _____ famiglia nobile.

9. L'italiano deriva _____ latino.

10. Ha copiato tutto il compito di matematica _____ suo vicino di banco.

Place Where, Motion Toward, and Motion From: *da (from)*

Italian uses **da** to convey *place where*, *motion toward*, and *motion from* when we mention the people and the social relations that occur in a place: **dai miei**, **dall'avvocato**.

Arrivo ora **dall'ufficio**.	*I just arrived **from work**.*
Torno ora **dall'avvocato**, che mi ha dato dei buoni consigli.	*I'm back **from talking to my lawyer**, who gave me good advice.*

Sentences such as «Vengo **dall'avvocato**» are ambiguous: am I joining someone else who is already at the lawyer's office, or am I coming back from the lawyer's office? In these cases, we add qualifiers that clarify the meaning.

Arrivo **da mia zia** tra dieci minuti.	*I'll be **at my aunt's** in ten minutes.*
Arrivo adesso **da casa di mia zia**.	*I'm just back **from my aunt's place**.*

esercizio   15-14

Translate the following sentences.

1. Luigi torna dall'università dopo le otto. _____

2. Vieni da casa di tuo fratello? _____

3. Vengo da mio fratello per cena. _____

4. Guarda, papà sta arrivando dalla farmacia con la medicina per te. _____

_____

5. Non voglio più andare da quel dentista. _____

6. Torno dal dentista perché il dente mi fa ancora male. _____

7. Non riesce a parlare perché è appena tornato dal dentista. _____

---

da, per, tra/fra (through, all around, and between/among)

Italian uses **da**, **per**, **tra/fra** to convey *motion through*. **Da** and **per** are often interchangeable. When followed by a name, they don't take the article.

Sono scappati **dall'uscita di emergenza**.	*They ran away **through the emergency exit**.*
Passiamo **per Vicenza** per andare a Ravenna?	*Shall we drive **through Vicenza** on our way to Ravenna?*

Tra/fra are used to convey movement when two or more places or points are involved.

Un raggio di sole passava **tra le lamelle delle veneziane**.	*A ray of sunlight entered the room **through the Venetian blinds**.*
Il fiume scorre **tra due catene montuose**.	*The river runs **between two mountain chains**.*

esercizio 15-15

*Add **da, per** or **tra/fra** to the following sentences. Add the definite article when needed.*

1. La nuova casa si trova _____ Genova e Livorno.

2. Sono passati _____ paese.

3. Mettete la crema pasticcera _____ due strati di sfoglia.

4. Ho viaggiato _____ tutta l'Europa.

5. L'ospite d'onore passa _____ porta principale.

6. I rapitori passarono _____ i boschi.

Qui, Qua, Lì, Là (Here and There)

Qui, qua, lì, là are adverbs of place. **Qui** and **qua** refer to a place close to speaker and listener; **lì** and **là** refer to a place far from both.

They can be introduced by the prepositions **di** and **da**, which convey *place where, motion toward, from, through, and origin*; and *motion toward, from, and through*.

Sono **di là**.	*They are **in the other room**.*
Arrivo adesso **da là**.	*I'm coming **from there** now.*

Additional Prepositions and Prepositional Locutions

accanto/vicino a	close/near to, by
al di sopra di; al di sotto di	above; beneath, underneath
dall'altra parte di...; attraverso	across, over, through
dal lato opposto di	opposite
davanti a	in front of, before
dentro; dentro a; all'interno di	in; inside; within
dietro; dietro a/di	behind; after
di fronte a	in front of, facing
fino a/da	as far as, as far away from
fuori; fuori di/da; al di fuori di	out/out of, outside, without
intorno a	around
lontano da	far (away) from
lungo	alongside
oltre; al di là di	beyond
verso	toward(s)

esercizio   15-16

Translate the following sentences, choosing among the prepositions and prepositional locutions listed above.

1. There were fifty journalists outside the courtroom. _____

_____

2. We strolled along the river. _____

3. They live far away from their family. _____

4. There is a flower shop across the street. _____

5. Sit close to me. _____

6. She was standing by the window. _____

7. No one had ever ventured beyond the mountains. (*avventurarsi*) _____

_____

8. The birds were all around the lake. _____

Time

Prepositions governing the expression of time behave in ways similar to prepositions we use to talk about space. Here follows a table of the **preposizioni semplici**.

di, a, in	days of the week; parts of the day/year, etc.; seasons
a, in	hours and minutes; holidays, named days
da, per	for X amount of time
in	sometime in a longer period
su	approximate point in time
in, su, per	length of time; for X amount of time
tra/fra	by a certain time
con	at the onset of

Moments in Time: *a* (*at*) and *di/in* (*in*)

A conveys a specific point in time, just as it does with space. It usually corresponds to the English *at*. Names of days and holidays do not take the definite article.

Vedrò la mia famiglia **a Natale**.	*I'll see my family **at Christmas**.*
Partiamo **alle sette**.	*We'll leave **at 7** A.M.*

Di and **in** are used to convey the idea of a chunk of time within which something happened, as **in** does when it comes to space.

Andiamo in vacanza **d'estate**.	*We go on vacation **in summer**.*
È nata **nel 1975**.	*She was born **in 1975**.*

Di is used without any article or determiner. **In** can be used with or without article or determiners. The definite article is added when we qualify the time we are talking about.

Le piace guidare **di notte**.	*She likes driving **at night**.*
Ti telefono **nella giornata di lunedì**.	*I'll call you **on Monday**.*

We can say **a marzo/in marzo**, but not **Parte delle/nelle sette**.

Ti vedo di/in Natale.

---

esercizio   16-1

Translate the following sentences.

1. A Pasqua ha fatto freddo. _____

2. L'ho visto l'ultima volta nel 1999. _____

3. D'inverno andiamo a sciare. _____

4. Si sono sposati nel mese di maggio. _____

5. A che ora partite? _____

6. Ad agosto fa molto caldo. _____

7. In agosto fa molto caldo. _____

8. A quest'ora dovrebbero essere già qui. _____

9. Marco veniva sempre a trovarci di sera. _____

---

esercizio   16-2

*Insert **a, di,** or **in** in the following sentences.*

1. Tutti si travestono _____ Carnevale.

2. Le lezioni incominciano _____ otto.

3. Le violette fioriscono _____ marzo.

4. La prima guerra mondiale scoppiò _____ 1914.

5. Nacque _____ una bella giornata di primavera.

6. Ha telefonato al medico _____ tre di mattina.

7. _____ domenica si va a messa.

8. Va a fare la spesa _____ pomeriggio.

esercizio   16-3

Translate the following sentences.

1. The train leaves at 10:30. _____

2. Sofia arrived (*è arrivata*) at night. _____

3. Do you (*sing.*) want to take that trip in September? _____

4. Kennedy was elected (*fu eletto*) president in 1960. _____

5. It's nice to go fishing on a warm summer day. _____

6. At Ferragosto all stores are closed. _____

7. He was born (*È nato*) in the nineteenth century! _____

8. Dinosaurs lived (*vissero*) in the quaternary. _____

Expressing Time Without Prepositions

We can often convey time without the help of a preposition.

Ci vediamo **la settimana prossima**.	*I'll see you **next week**.*
Siamo a casa **tutte le sere**.	*We're home **every evening**.*
Giochiamo a tennis **sabato**?	*Shall we play tennis **this Saturday**?*
È nata **il 21 marzo 1952**.	*She was born (**on**) **March 21, 1952**.*
Gli ho parlato **un Natale di tanti anni fa**.	*I talked to him **on Christmas day many years ago**.*

esercizio   16-4

Translate the following sentences.

1. Andiamo a cavallo il prossimo fine settimana. _____

2. Sei libero stamattina? _____

3. Sono rimasti da noi tutto il giorno. _____

4. Ricomincio a lavorare martedì. _____

5. I gemelli sono nati nel 1985, il 10 agosto. _____

6. Un giorno ci incontreremo di nuovo. _____

7. Che cosa fai il prossimo sabato? _____

8. La settimana scorsa sono stata al mare. _____

Di Domenica/la Domenica (on Sundays); Domenica ([on] Sunday, This Coming Sunday)

In Italian **di domenica** and **la domenica** mean *on Sundays*, whereas **domenica** means *this coming Sunday*.

La domenica fa piacere dormire fino a tardi.	*It's nice to sleep late **on Sundays**.*
Di domenica si finisce per non fare niente di interessante.	***On Sundays** one ends up doing nothing interesting.*
Verremo a trovarvi **domenica**, promesso.	*We'll come visit you **this Sunday**, it's a promise.*

esercizio   16-5

*Insert the proper prepositions in the following sentences, when one is needed. Choose among **a**, **in**, **di**.*

1. Passerò da te _____ sabato.

2. Passa da lei _____ tutti i sabati.

3. È nato _____ lunedì.

4. Vanno a ginnastica _____ martedì.

5. Partiremo per la Nuova Zelanda _____ novembre, non so ancora il giorno.

6. Vi siete divertiti _____ Capodanno?

7. Siete arrivati _____ un'ora impossibile. Ma dove siete stati?

8. Non si semina _____ gennaio!

9. È nato _____ il 15 maggio.

10. Sono morti tutti _____ 1998, in quel terribile incidente.

From the Past to the Present: *da (for and since/from)*

Da is used to convey the idea that something started in the past and is continuing to the present moment (English *for*), and to indicate the starting point of actions (English *since* or *from*).

Studia il flauto **da tre anni**.	*He's been studying the flute **for three years**.*
Aspetto **dalle sei**!	*I've been waiting **since six o'clock**!*
Non li vediamo **dal 1998**.	*We haven't seen them **since 1998**.*
Non li vediamo **da molto tempo**.	*We haven't seen them **for a long time**.*

To convey the point in time in the future when something *will* start, Italian uses **da** (*from*) or **a partire da** (*starting from*) a certain time, or **da... in poi** (*after* a certain time).

Elena sarà in ufficio **dalle tre/ a partire dalle tre**.

Giorgio sarà a casa **dalle sette in poi**.

Elena will be in the office from/starting at three o'clock.

Giorgio will be gone from 7 P.M. onward.

When we refer to a *period of time* in the past, we use the **imperfetto** (*simple past*).

Quando lo conobbi **suonava** la chitarra **da tre anni**.

*When I met him **he had been playing the guitar for three years**.*

When we refer to a period of time in the past which is lasting to this moment, Italian uses **il presente indicativo** (*simple present*), whereas English uses either the *present perfect* or *the present perfect progressive*.

---

esercizio	16-6

Translate the following sentences.

1. I work from nine to five. _____

2. I've known her since January. _____

3. The house has been empty since March. _____

4. Nicola has been dating (*uscire con*) Paola for five years. _____

   _____

5. We have been selling furnaces since 1925. _____

6. The doctor will be available starting at four. _____

7. Starting Monday, the store will close at 9 P.M. _____

8. I've known her since our childhood. _____

---

per (for)

Italian distinguishes between events or actions that *lasted for a time but ended*, and events that *started in the past and continue to this day*. As seen, the latter is expressed with the preposition **da**. *Events that are over* or *periods of time in the future* are conveyed with the preposition **per**.

When we refer to the past, the verb is now commonly in the **passato prossimo** (*simple present perfect*), rather than the **passato remoto** (*simple past*). When we refer to the future, the verb can be in the **presente indicativo** (*simple present*) or **futuro** (*future*).

Ha studiato la chitarra **per tre anni**.
Andremo/Andiamo in vacanza
   per due settimane.
Non li abbiamo visti **per molto tempo**.

*He studied the guitar **for three years**.*
We'll go on vacation
   ***for two weeks**.*
*We didn't see them **for a long time**.*

The preposition **per** can be omitted when we talk about duration.

Ha studiato la chitarra **tre anni**.
Staremo via **tre mesi**.

*He studied the guitar **three years**.*
*We'll be away **three months**.*

Per can also convey an action repeated every X amount of time, or a deadline.

Suona il piano **per otto ore al giorno**.
Ti prometto che sarò a casa **per le sei**.
L'appuntamento è stato fissato
   per le due e mezza.

*She plays the piano **eight hours a day**.*
*I promise you I'll be home **by six**.*
The appointment was set
   ***for 2:30**.*

esercizio 16-7

Translate the following sentences.

1. Elisa studied (*ha studiato*) all night. _____

2. Elisa will study only anatomy for two weeks. _____

3. I worked with Paolo for five years. _____

4. She works with my sister four hours a day. _____

5. She will work with my sister for four hours. _____

6. My mother studied piano for ten years. _____

7. Her aunt studied English for three years. _____

8. She will study English for six months in Australia. _____

esercizio 16-8

*Insert **da** or **per** in the following sentences. You also have the option of not inserting anything.*

1. Non ci parliamo più _____ mesi.

2. Non gli ho parlato _____ dei mesi.

3. Non gli parlo _____ notte di Capodanno del 2000.

4. Irma parla con Angelo al telefono _____ un'ora ogni giorno.

5. Resteremo negli Stati Uniti _____ cinque anni.

6. Si è presa cura di suo marito _____ cinque anni.

7. Siamo sposati _____ dieci anni.

8. Sono proprio stanca. Andiamo in vacanza _____ una settimana?

9. Siamo stati sposati _____ dieci anni.

10. Non la vedo _____ lunedì.

How Long It Takes: *in, tra,* and *entro* (*in, by,* and *within*)

When we wish to convey how soon something will happen, or how long something takes to happen, we use **in**, **tra**, and **entro**.

In corresponds to the English *in* when it conveys *how long* something takes to happen.

L'ho fatto **in tre giorni**.	*I did it **in three days**.*

Tra and **entro** convey the English *in* when used to indicate the *end* of the period of time it takes for something to happen.

Sarà finito **tra/entro due settimane**.	*It will be finished **two weeks from today/within two weeks**.*
Lo finisco **tra dieci giorni**.	*I'll finish it **in ten days**.*

Tra can also be used to mean *between*.

Vengono a trovarci **tra Natale e Pasqua**.	*They will come visit us **between Christmas and Easter**.*

Entro is used to convey the idea of *no later than*, when we give a specific deadline.

Sarà finito **entro sabato**.	*It will be done **by Saturday**.*
[*Not*: Sarà finito **tra sabato**.]	
Sarà finito **entro il 15 luglio**.	*It will be done **by July 15**.*

When we know the exact time when something will be done, we can say:

Sarà pronto **sabato**.	*It will be ready **Saturday**.*

Note: **In orario** translates as *on time*, **in tempo** as *in time*.

Il volo era **in orario**.	*The flight was **on time**.*
Siamo arrivati **in tempo**.	*We got there **in time**.*

esercizio	16-9

*Translate the following sentences. Use **in**, **tra**, and **entro**.*

1. We are leaving (*simple pres.*) by Thursday. _____

2. We are leaving Thursday. _____

3. Is she coming back in two years? _____

4. She will marry him by the end of the year. _____

5. She will marry him by December 20. _____

6. They will be divorced within a year. _____

7. I'll be home by five o'clock. _____

8. "Can I borrow (*prendere*) your car?" "Yes, but I must have it back by tonight."

_____

Adverbs Used as Prepositions: *prima di (before)* and *dopo (di) (after)*

The adverbs **prima** (*before*) and **dopo** (*after*) can be used as prepositions. **Prima** is always followed by the preposition **di**. **Dopo** needs **di** if it precedes a pronoun.

Telefonami **prima di cena**.	*Call me **before dinner**.*
Ti telefono **dopo cena**.	*I'll call you **after dinner**.*
Hanno decollato **prima di noi**.	*They took off **before us**.*
Arrivate sempre **dopo di lei**.	*You always arrive **after her**.*

Italian uses **prima** and **dopo** to convey *position in place* and *position in time* at the same time, for example when we talk about people being in line.

Ero **prima di** lei nella coda.	*I was **ahead of** her. / I was **first**. /*
	*I was **before her** in line.*

esercizio	16-10

Translate the following sentences.

1. Ti telefonerò prima della partenza. _____

2. Ci vediamo dopo pranzo. _____

3. Lo avrai prima di sera. _____

4. Luca arriverà dopo il tramonto. _____

5. Hanno rinviato la discussione a dopo cena. _____

6. Prego, dopo di lei, Signora. _____

7. Torni prima di domani? _____

8. Sono spariti uno dopo l'altro. _____

9. C'è Lei prima di me. _____

10. Dopo di te nessuno si prenderà cura del giardino. _____

Purpose, Company, and Agency

In this section we consider the prepositions that help us convey the following ideas: that someone else is the *recipient* of what we do; that we have a *purpose* in acting; that we do something *with someone*; and that actions are carried out *by someone* or *something*.

a (to) and *per (for)*

Since an action addressed to someone or something else conveys a "movement" of a kind, we use prepositions that signal *motion toward*: **a** (*to*) and **per** (*for*).

Ho dato il mio libro **a Sandro**.	*I gave my book **to Sandro**.*
Ho comprato il caviale **per mio padre**.	*I bought caviar **for my father**.*

With the weak pronouns **mi**, **ti**, **gli**, ecc., the preposition *a* (*to*) and **per** (*for*) are dropped (see Unit 3).

Gli ho comprato il pane.   *I bought the bread **for him**.*

esercizio   17-1

Translate the following sentences.

1. Ha portato (*to give*) dei cioccolatini a sua zia.

   _____

2. Avete spedito la domanda all'ufficio iscrizioni dell'università?

   _____

3. Gli ho dato tutti i miei soldi. Li investirà lui per me. _____

_____

4. Hai comprato il latte per il gatto? _____

5. Hanno consegnato un pacco per tuo padre. _____

_____

6. Hanno consegnato un pacco a tuo padre. _____

_____

7. Gli hanno mandato un pacco. _____

8. Abbiamo detto la verità a Lucia. _____

9. Chiedilo a Roberto. _____

10. Ha combattuto per la libertà del suo paese. _____

_____

esercizio   17-2

Translate the following sentences. Indirect object pronouns are used without prepositions.

1. She has made (*ha fatto*) great sacrifices for her children. _____

_____

2. In that museum you can see old machinery (*macchinari*) for the production of silk. _____

_____

3. We gave (*abbiamo regalato*) her my mother's jewelry. _____

_____

4. They gave (*hanno dato*) my mother's jewelry to her and not to me. _____

_____

5. They do a lot of volunteer work for orphan children. _____

_____

6. "Does speleology interest you?" "No, it doesn't interest me." _____

_____

7. The U.N. is accepting contributions for the victims of the tsunami. _____

_____

8. What did you (*sing.*) do to your clothes? _____

_____

con, insieme con/a (with)

When we wish to convey the idea that we are doing something *together with someone else*, Italian and English use similar prepositions and prepositional locutions.

Vado al cinema **con mio fratello**.   *I'm going to the movies **with my brother**.*
Lucia sta sempre **insieme a Pietro**.   *Lucia is always **with Pietro**.*

Con can also be used to mean **contro** (*against*).

La guerra **con la Cina** durò dieci anni.   *The war **with China** lasted ten years.*

esercizio   **17-3**

Translate the following sentences.

1. Gianna prende lezioni di sci con sua cugina. _____

_____

2. Il mio cane gioca sempre insieme al suo (*di lei*) gatto. _____

_____

3. Sandra ha preso un appuntamento con il medico.

_____

4. Federico arriva tutte le sere al bar in compagnia di uno strano tipo.

_____

5. Faremo un viaggio insieme a dei nostri vecchi amici.

_____

6. Con chi vai a cena? _____

_____

7. Con te non si può parlare. _____

_____

esercizio   17-4

Translate the following sentences.

1. He got engaged to a Japanese woman. _____

_____

2. My son still sleeps with his teddy bear (*orsacchiotto di peluche*). _____

_____

3. Nadia is coming to the hairdresser with you. _____

_____

4. If you (*sing.*) work together with your brother, business will get (*andranno*) better. _____

_____

5. I'm always at ease with him. _____

_____

6. I always see Francesca in the company of her college professor. _____

_____

7. That old lady lives with thirty cats. _____

_____

da (*by*) and the Passive Voice

da is used to convey the agent *by whom/which* the action is performed when the verb is in the passive voice.

Amleto è stato scritto **da Shakespeare**.   Hamlet *was written* **by Shakespeare**.
Il paese è stato distrutto **dalla frana**.   *The town was destroyed* **by the landslide**.

esercizio	17-5

Translate the following sentences.

1. I (*masc.*) was interviewed by three film directors. _____

2. My car was damaged by a tree branch (*ramo*). _____

_____

3. She was not loved by her children. _____

4. The hotel was buried by the avalanche. _____

5. Gaul was (*fu*) conquered by Julius Caesar. _____

6. The milk was spilled by the cat. _____

7. Renato was bitten by a snake. _____

da + the Infinitive

Italian uses **da** + *verb in the present infinitive* to convey the idea that something *is to be done* or *can be done*. **Da** + *verb* carries four different meanings:

- Something is available for us to do.

  «Hai dei libri **da leggere**»?   *"Do you have any books **to read**?"*
  «Non preoccuparti, ho tutti   *"Don't worry. I have as many*
    quelli che voglio».   *as I want."*

- Something must be done.

  Il professore ci ha dato **da leggere**   *The professor assigned three books **for us***
    tre libri.   ***to read**.*

- Something needs to be done.

  La mia automobile è **da lavare**.   My car needs **washing**.

- Something is worth doing.

  È un posto **da vedere**.   *It's a place **worth seeing**.*

esercizio   17-6

Translate the following sentences.

1. Vuoi qualcosa da mangiare? _____

2. Ho molto da fare. _____

3. Non ho niente da fare. _____

4. Puoi darmi qualcosa da bere? _____

5. Quello è un film da vedere. _____

6. Ho la cena da preparare. _____

7. Mio nonno non ha più molto tempo da vivere. _____

_____

esercizio   17-7

Translate the following sentences.

1. What do you (*sing.*) have to do? _____

2. The robber had many crimes to confess. _____

3. The policeman has three cases that must be solved. _____

_____

4. They have nothing to say to each other. _____

5. That blouse needs washing. _____

6. After so many discussions, the bridge is still to be built. _____

_____

7. Three condos (*appartamenti*) are still to be sold. _____

_____

Means, Qualities, and Causes

In this section we consider the prepositions that convey what *tool* we employ to get something done; what *characteristics* someone or something possesses; and the *reasons* or *causes* that explain why something has happened.

Means: *con* and *in* (*with*)

We use **con** (*with*) to convey *the tool with which we get something done.*

Ho ucciso il ragno **con una scarpa**.	*I killed the spider **with a shoe**.*

Note: We use **da** when we indicate the tool that *performed* the action.

È stato ucciso **da una valanga**.	*He was killed **by an avalanche**.*

When the *tool* is a *means of transportation*, Italian uses both **con** and **in**; English mostly uses *by*. **Con** is always used with the article, either separate from it (**con il, la, lo, i, gli, le**), or as a **preposizione articolata** (**col, coi**). **In** is used without an article.

Vengo **in bici**. / Vengo **con la bici**.	*I'm coming **by bike**.*
Arriva **in treno**.	*He's arriving **by train**.*

esercizio	18-1

*Translate the following sentences. Use **in**.*

1. We're going to Moscow by train. _____

_____

2. I go to work by bike. _____

3. She always travels by plane. _____

4. Is it better to go to Milan by train or by car? _____

5. They crossed (*hanno attraversato*) the Atlantic Ocean by boat. _____

_____

6. The rebels fled (*scapparono*) by helicopter. _____

7. We will go around the world by ship. _____

8. Are you (*pl.*) touring (*girare per*) the countryside by motorbike? _____

_____

> We say **in treno**, **in macchina**, **in aereo**, **in nave**, **in bici**, **in moto**, **in barca a vela**, ecc., *but* **a piedi** (*on foot*), **a cavallo** (*on a horse*), **sui pattini** (*on skates*); **per posta** (*by mail*); **via/tramite e-mail** (*via/ by e-mail*).

esercizio	18-2

Translate the following sentences.

1. Mia madre ha pulito il tappeto con l'aceto. _____

2. Che azioni hai comprato con i soldi di tua moglie? _____

3. Anna si è coperta la testa con una sciarpa. _____

4. Il mio gatto gioca con la corda delle tende. _____

5. Non riuscirai ad abbattere quell'albero con questa sega. _____

_____

6. Con la bicicletta non andate lontano. _____

7. Arriviamo in centro prima con la metropolitana. _____

8. Hanno annunciato la fine della guerra con un messaggio alla radio. _____

_____

esercizio	18-3

Translate the following sentences. Use **con**.

1. Are you (*sing.*) going from London to Rome by train?

_____

2. With my grandfather's inheritance I'm buying a cottage (*casetta*) on the sea.

_____

3. Nomads used to cross (*attraversavano*) the desert by camel.

_____

4. I will answer your (*pl.*) questions with a letter.

_____

5. Silvia likes pasta with butter and parmesan.

_____

6. It's juice made with oranges from her orchard.

_____

7. Troy was taken with a fake horse.

_____

8. He likes roaming (*girare per*) the countryside by motorbike.

_____

con (*with*) and Means of Transportation

When we qualify or specify some feature of the means of transportation we are using, Italian uses **con**, as English uses *with*.

Arrivo **col treno delle dieci**.   *I will arrive **with the 10 A.M. train**.*
  [*Not*: Arrivo **in treno delle dieci**.]
Si sposta **con la macchina della ditta**.   *He moves around **with his firm's car**.*
  [*Not*: Si sposta **in macchina della ditta**.]

18-4

Translate the following sentences.

1. Preferiscono viaggiare con una macchina a noleggio.

   _____

2. Ada parte con l'aereo delle ventuno.

   _____

3. Massimo viene con la moto nuova.

   _____

4. Hanno fatto il giro del mondo con la barca a vela che ha vinto l'America's Cup.

   _____

5. Volete andare in Cina con quel camion?!

   _____

6. Con la bici da corsa faccio trenta chilometri all'ora.

   _____

esercizio   18-5

Translate the following sentences.

1. I will fly (*simple pres.*) to New York with the 5 P.M. plane.

   _____

2. Isabella goes shopping (*andare a fare la spesa*) with her father's Rolls-Royce.

   _____

3. Do you want to climb (*andare su*) Mount McKinley with your mountain bike?

   _____

4. My brother drives around (*andare in giro per*) town with his new Hummer.

   _____

5. With the 8 A.M. train we'll get to Manhattan at 10:30.

_____

6. They're sending (*simple pres.*) the astronauts to the moon with an old rocket.

_____

Insert **in** *or* **con** *in the following sentences. Both may be correct. The less idiomatic answer is given in brackets in the* answer section.

1. D'estate vado a lavorare _____ bici.

2. _____ questa nave spaziale non arriveremo mai su Arturo.

3. Siamo andati in Russia _____ moto.

4. Ha vinto la corsa _____ la moto di suo zio.

5. Voglio attraversare l'Alaska _____ treno.

6. La Vasaloppet è una gara che si fa _____ gli sci da fondo.

7. Ha attraversato la Siberia d'inverno _____ slitta.

8. Riuscite a fare cinquanta chilometri al giorno _____ bici?

Functions and Characteristics: *barche a vela* and *carte da gioco*

Italian uses **a** to introduce a prepositional phrase expressing what *tool* an object employs to perform its function.

Hanno comprato **una barca a vela**.   *They bought **a sailing boat**.*

It uses **da** + *noun* or *verb in the infinitive* to express the *purpose* for which an object is used. In most cases, English conveys purpose by inverting the word order.

Hai portato il **costume da bagno?**   *Did you bring a **bathing suit**?*

Below is a list of common objects that follow this pattern.

Means
_____

la barca a motore	motorboat
la centrale a carbone	coal plant
la cucina a gas	gas stove
il motore a scoppio	internal combustion engine

il mulino a vento	windmill
lo strumento a corda	stringed instrument
lo strumento a fiato	wind instrument
lo strumento a percussione	percussion instrument
la stufa a legna	wood stove

esercizio   18-7

Add the appropriate prepositional phrase to the following sentences.

1. Gli ecologisti sono contrari alle _____ perché sono molto inquinanti.

2. Il pianoforte è uno _____; il clavicembalo è uno strumento a corda.

3. Stiamo riscoprendo _____, perché usano una fonte di energia rinnovabile.

4. _____ italiane non hanno mai vinto l'America's Cup.

5. Finalmente mi sono liberata della cucina elettrica e ne ho installata una

   _____.

Purpose

l'abito da sera	evening gown
l'asse da stiro	ironing board
il bicchiere da acqua/da vino	water/wine glass
la bicicletta da corsa	racing bike
il biglietto da visita	business card
la camera da letto/sala da pranzo	bedroom/dining room
la camicia da notte	night robe
il cane da caccia/guardia/pastore	hunting/guard/shepherd dog
la canna da pesca	fishing rod
la carta da musica	music paper
le carte da gioco	playing cards
il cavallo da corsa	racehorse
il ferro da stiro	iron
la festa da ballo	dance, ball
la macchina da corsa	racing car
la macchina da scrivere	typewriter
la musica da camera	chamber music
gli occhiali da sole	sunglasses
la pallina da golf/tennis	golf/tennis ball
la pentola da forno	ovenproof pot/Dutch oven
il piatto da minestra/pietanza	soup bowl/flat plate
il piattino da insalata/frutta/dolce	salad/fruit/dessert plate
la racchetta da tennis	tennis racket
le racchette da neve	snow shoes
le scarpe da tennis	tennis shoes
gli scarponi da roccia/sci	rock-climbing/ski boots
gli sci da fondo	cross-country skis

il tavolino/comodino da notte	nightstand/table
la tazzina da caffé	demitasse
la tazza da tè	teacup

---

esercizio   18-8

Add the appropriate prepositional phrase to the following sentences.

1. Non gli piace il computer. Usa ancora una vecchia _____ manuale!

2. Stasera mangiamo solo il secondo e il dolce. Non c'è bisogno dei _____.

3. Vince sempre a poker perchè usa _____ truccate.

4. Non andare sul ghiacciaio senza _____, può farti male agli occhi.

5. Da bambini avevamo un _____, perchè mio padre era un cacciatore.

6. Vuoi una mountain bike o una _____?

7. Per l'ingresso in società della figlia daranno una _____ con trecento invitati.

8. Sono andata al mare senza _____, così ho nuotato nuda.

9. Carlo insiste a giocare a golf, ma perde sempre _____ nel bosco.

10. Ho dato il mio _____ al direttore della banca. Spero che mi dia un lavoro.

Qualities

In Italian, most **preposizioni semplici** can be used to convey the idea that we do something *in a certain manner,* or that things and people have certain *qualities.* In English, *in* and *with* are the most common. In many cases, a *preposition + noun construction conveying manner* can be turned into an *adverb* in both Italian and English.

Si è spiegato **con grande chiarezza**.	*He explained himself **with great clarity**.*
Si è spiegato **molto chiaramente**.	*He explained himself **very clearly**.*

Given the array of prepositions that can be used in both languages to *convey the way in which something is done* or *the qualities things possess or exhibit,* it seems helpful to provide students with lists of prepositional phrases and their English equivalents.

Prepositional Phrases with *di*

d'un fiato	in one breath
di buon passo	at a good clip
di corsa	running
di cuore	wholeheartedly
di fretta	in a hurry
di gusto	willingly; with pleasure

di magro	(to eat) light
di malavoglia	unwillingly
di rosso	in red

esercizio   18-9

Add the appropriate prepositional phrase to the following sentences.

1. Mio marito ha dipinto tutta la casa, ma l'ha fatto proprio _____.

2. È arrivata _____ perchè pensava di essere in ritardo.

3. Mangia _____ per dimagrire.

4. Ti vesti sempre _____?

5. Non posso parlarti adesso. Sono _____.

Prepositional Phrases with **a**

a caso	randomly
a credito	on credit
a dirotto	(raining) cats and dogs
a bassa voce	in a low voice
a malincuore	regretfully
a memoria	by heart
a olio	oil (painting)
a voce bassa	in a low voice
ad acquerello	in watercolors
ad alta voce	in a high/loud voice
al minuto	retail
all'antica	old-fashioned
all'ingrosso	wholesale
alla rinfusa	helter-skelter
(fatto) a macchina	machine made
(fatto) a mano	handmade
(scrivere) a macchina	to type
(scrivere) a mano	to write by hand
(scrivere) a stampatello	to print

esercizio   18-10

Add the appropriate prepositional phrase to the following sentences.

1. Non dipinge più a olio, solo _____.

2. Ettore parla sempre _____, non capisco mai niente.

3. Queste scarpe costano un sacco di soldi perché sono _____.

4. Siete pregati di compilare il modulo scrivendo _____.

5. Nessuno dei corsi mi interessa particolarmente, così ho scelto _____.

6. Ha imparato tutte le tragedie di Shakespeare _____.

7. Comprano tutto _____. Uno di questi giorni faranno bancarotta.

8. I prezzi _____ sono stabili, ma al mercato quelli _____ sono saliti del 3 percento in un mese.

A is also used to add a qualifier to an object. English adds a noun, or a present or past participle working as adjectives.

Porta solo **le maglie a girocollo**.	*She only wears **crewneck sweaters**.*
Le piacciono **le gonne a pieghe**.	*She likes **pleated skirts**.*
Il soggiorno è piccolo: ci sta solo **un sofa a due posti**.	*The living room is small. There is only room for **a love seat**.*

Clothing: Prepositional Phrases with **a**

la borsa a tracolla	shoulder-strap bag
il cappello a larghe tese	wide-brimmed hat
la gonna a pieghe	pleated skirt
il letto a castello	bunk bed
la maglia a collo alto	high-neck sweater
la maglia a girocollo	round-neck sweater
i pantaloni a sigaretta	pencil pants
i pantaloni a zampa di elefante	bell-bottom pants
i pantaloni alla pescatora	Capri pants
le scarpe a punta	pointed shoes
le scarpe col tacco a spillo	stiletto shoes
la scollatura a V	V-neck cut
la sedia a dondolo	rocking chair
il sofa a due/tre posti	love seat/three-seat sofa

esercizio 18-11

Add the appropriate prepositional phrase to the following sentences.

1. Il podologo dice che _____ danneggiano le dita dei piedi.

2. Mio nonno passa tutte le sue serate seduto davanti al fuoco sulla sua _____.

3. In quel collegio alle bambine non lasciano portare i pantaloni, solo _____.

4. Portava _____ che gli nascondeva quasi tutto il viso.

5. Mi piacciono molto i pantaloni _____, che erano di moda negli anni cinquanta.

Qualities can also be introduced with the prepositions **da**, **con**, **in**, or **per**.

Prepositional Phrases with **da**

da adulto/da grande	as a grown-up/responsibly
da amico	as a friend
da bambino	childishly
da esperto	expertly
da imbecille	like an imbecile
da galantuomo	like a gentleman
da principiante	like a greenhorn
dall'aria sospetta	suspiciously
da persona educata	politely
da vecchio	as an old person
dai capelli biondi	with blonde hair
dalla voce forte	with a strong voice
dalla volontà ferrea	with an iron will

Note: The expressions **da adulto/da grande**, **da bambino**, **da vecchio**, ecc., can also mean *when you're grown up, when you were a child, when you're old.*

Da grande voglio fare il pompiere.   ***When I grow up*** *I want to be a firefighter.*

esercizio   18-12

Add the appropriate prepositional phrase to the following sentences.

1. Con me il Signor Calandri si è sempre comportato _____.

2. Ho visto un uomo _____ dietro casa e ho chiamato la polizia.

3. Sandro, non mettere le scarpe sul tavolo! Comportati _____.

4. C'era una ragazza _____, ma non era Vittoria.

5. Non ci ho guadagnato niente a trattarti _____.

Prepositional Phrases with **con**

con il fiato corto	with bated breath
con calma	calmly
con cautela/prudenza	cautiously/prudently
con certezza	with certainty
con chiarezza	with clarity; clearly
con cura	with care; carefully
con impegno	earnestly
con intelligenza	intelligently
con la verdura	with vegetables
con le mani nel sacco	red-handed
con leggerezza	lightly; superficially
con onestà	honestly

con passione	with passion; passionately
con precisione	precisely
con senso dell'umorismo	with a sense of humor
con serietà	seriously
con tutto il cuore	with all one's heart; wholeheartedly

esercizio 18-13

Add the appropriate prepositional phrase to the following sentences.

1. Fai le cose _____, abbiamo tutto il tempo necessario.

2. Hai agito _____ non investendo i soldi in quell'affare.

3. Ti sei comportata _____ parlando in pubblico degli affari del tuo cliente.

4. Abbiamo una perdita nel tetto, la macchina è rotta e mio figlio ha perso le chiavi di casa, ma noi prendiamo tutto _____.

5. Ti auguro _____ di trovare la persona giusta per te.

6. Abbiamo fatto le cose _____, eppure ci sono ancora degli errori.

7. Sono arrivati _____, ma almeno sono riusciti a non perdere il treno.

Prepositional Phrases with **in**

in bianco	in white/wearing white; to eat light
in cerchio	in a circle
in coda	in line
in contanti	cash
in due, quattro, cento, ecc.	it's two, four, one hundred, etc.
in dubbio	in doubt
in fila indiana	in single file
in ordine alfabetico	in alphabetical order
in pace	at peace
in punta di piedi	on tiptoe
in saldo	on sale
in silenzio	silently; quietly
in vendita	for sale

esercizio 18-14

Add the appropriate prepositional phrase to the following sentences.

1. Al matrimonio c'erano almeno tre signore _____ come la sposa.

2. Marianna è _____ se accettare quel lavoro o no.

3. Bambini, non potete camminare tutti insieme, mettetevi _____.

4. Ci siamo fatti tutti _____ a dare una mano, quando c'è stata l'alluvione.

5. Ti ringrazio di aver messo le cartelline _____. C'era una tale confusione!

6. Lascia _____ tua sorella, non vedi che ha tanti compiti da fare?

7. Mangia _____ da una vita, per quello è così magro.

8. In quel ristorante non accettano carte di credito o assegni; si paga solo _____.

9. Il vestito che costava trecento euro adesso ne costa solo centocinquanta perché è

_____.

Prepositional Phrases with **per/su**

per filo e per segno	to the last detail
per gioco	in jest
per nome	by first name
per ordine alfabetico	in alphabetical order
per scherzo	in jest
per scritto	in writing
su misura/ordinazione	made to order
sulla Bibbia/sul Vangelo	on the Bible/Gospel
sulla parola	at someone's word
stare sulle sue	to be standoffish

esercizio   18-15

Add the appropriate prepositional phrase to the following sentences.

1. Ma dai, non prendertela, l'ho detto _____!

2. Mi ha creduto _____ e mi ha dato il prestito.

3. Il mio avvocato ha voluto che mettessimo tutto _____.

4. Suo zio non ha mai comprato un abito fatto in vita sua. Si fa fare tutto _____.

5. Le due amichette si chiusero in camera e si raccontarono tutto _____.

6. Il testimone è ateo. Si rifiuta di giurare _____.

7. L'ho chiamato _____, ma ha fatto finta di non conoscermi.

Causes: *di, a, con, da, in, per (of, at, with, in, from, for)*

When we want to say that something *caused* something else, or give *reasons for* what happened, English and Italian use an array of prepositions. Here follows some examples. **Di** is used without the definite article; other prepositions are accompanied by it.

Tremava **dalla paura**.	*He was trembling **with fear**.*
Saltava **dalla gioia**.	*She was jumping **for joy**.*
Moriva **di fame**.	*She was dying **from hunger**.*
Soffrono **di nostalgia**.	*They suffer **from nostalgia**.*
Con questo caldo, è difficile lavorare.	***With this heat** it's hard to work.*
Con l'inflazione che c'è, il mio stipendio non vale più niente.	***With inflation** so high, my salary isn't worth anything any longer.*
Con tutto il lavoro che ho, non potrò andare al cinema stasera.	***With all the work** I have to do, I won't be able to go to the movies tonight.*
Con tre persone assenti dall'ufficio, dobbiamo lavorare il doppio.	***With three people** away from the office, we have to work twice as hard.*
Tremava **per il freddo**.	*She was shivering **with cold**.*
Soffrono **per la lontananza**.	*They suffer **because they are so far away**.*

Il gerundio: by + the *-ing* Form

When we talk about the performance of an action that has led to a certain result, in Italian we can use:

- **il gerundio**. English mostly uses *by* + *-ing* form (or *by* + a noun).

È diventato ricco **lavorando sodo**.	*He got rich **by hard work/by working hard**.*

- **per** + *the past infinitive* to talk about *an action that has led to a certain result*. English uses *for* + *-ing* form.

È stato punito **per aver rotto la finestra** a scuola.	*He was punished **for breaking** the window at school.*

There are other prepositions and prepositional phrases that can be used to convey means, as follows.

Other Prepositional Phrases

a/per causa di	because of
a favore di	in favor of
attraverso/tramite	through
grazie a	thanks to
per colpa di	to be someone's fault if . . .
per conto di	on behalf of
per il bene di	for the sake/good of
per mezzo di	by means of
per opera di	thanks to/by

esercizio	18-16

*Add the appropriate prepositional phrase to the following sentences. Use **preposizioni articolate** if necessary.*

1. I senatori dell'opposizione voteranno _____ legge contro il fumo.

2. I dissidenti hanno ottenuto asilo politico _____ l'intervento dell'ONU.

3. Abbiamo perso tutti i soldi _____ un consulente finanziario disonesto.

4. _____ la pioggia abbiamo dovuto rimandare la gita.

5. Non hanno divorziato _____ i loro figli.

Tables of Pronouns

Subject and Direct Object Pronouns

Subject pronouns (Pronomi soggetto)		Direct object pronouns (Complemento oggetto)		Personal pronouns (Pronomi personali)
I	io	me	mi	me
you	tu	you	ti	te
he	egli/lui	him	lo	lui
she	ella/lei	her	la	lei
it	esso/essa	it	lo/la	—
we	noi	us	ci	noi
you	voi	you	vi	voi
they	essi/esse/loro	them	li/le	loro

Indirect Object Pronouns

Complemento di termine Weak form (to/for someone: **a**)		Other indirect objects (*Altri complementi*) Strong form (by, with, to, etc.; **da, con, a**, *ecc.*)	
me	mi	me	me
you	ti	te	te
him	gli	lui	lui
her	le	lei	lei
us	ci	noi	noi
you	vi	voi	voi
them	(gli)	loro/loro	loro

Double pronouns		Reflexive pronouns		Double/reflexive pronouns	
him/her, etc., to me	**me lo/la**, ecc.	myself	**mi**	**me lo/la**, ecc.	
him/her, etc., to you	**te**	yourself	**ti**	**te lo**	
him/her, etc., to him	**glielo**	himself	**si**	**se lo**	
him/her, etc., to her	**glielo**	herself	**si**	**se lo**	
		itself	**si**	**se lo**	
		oneself	**si**	**se lo**	
him/her, etc., to us	**ce lo**	ourselves	**ce**	**ce lo**	
him/her, etc., to you	**ve lo**	yourselves	**vi**	**ve lo**	
him/her, etc., to them	**glielo**	themselves	**si**	**se lo**	

Interrogative Pronouns (Pronomi Interrogativi)

who/whom	**chi**
whose	**di chi**
to/for/by, etc., whom	**a/per/da chi**

what	**che/che cosa**
what/which	**quale/quali**
how much/many	**quanto/a/i/e**

Relative Pronouns (Pronomi Relativi)

	Invariable	Variable
who	**che**	**il quale, la quale, i quali, le quali**
whom	**che**	**il quale, la quale, i quali, le quali**
that	**che**	**il quale, la quale, i quali, le quali**
which	**che**	**il quale, la quale, i quali, le quali**
whose/of which	**di cui/il cui**	**del quale, della quale, dei quali, delle quali**
to/for whom/which	**cui; a/per cui**	**al/per il quale, alla quale, ai quali, alle quali**
from, in, by, etc., whom/which	**da, in, cui**	**per il quale, dal quale, nel quale,** ecc.

Demonstrative Pronouns (Pronomi Dimostrativi)

this/these	**questo/a, questi/e**
that/those	**quello/a, quelle/i**
this/that	**ciò**

Possessive Pronouns (Pronomi Possessivi)

mine	**il mio/la mia/i miei/le mie**
yours	**il tuo/la tua/i tuoi/le tue**
his, hers, its	**il suo/la sua/i suoi/le sue**
ours	**il nostro/la nostra/i nostri/le nostre**
yours	**il vostro/la vostra/i vostri/le vostre**
theirs	**il loro/la loro/i loro/le loro**

Indefinite Pronouns (Pronomi Indefiniti)

alcuni, alcune/qualcuno	some/any/a few
altro	else
un altro, un'altra/gli altri, le altre	another/(the) others
chiunque	anyone/anybody
ciascuno, ciascuna/ognuno, ognuna	each/everyone
gli uni... gli altri/le une... le altre	some . . . the others
l'un l'altro, l'un l'altra	each other/one another
molti, molte	many/a lot
molto, molta	much
nessuno	no one/nobody
niente/nulla	nothing
parecchi, parecchie	a lot/several
pochi, poche	a little/too little/few
poco, poca	a little/too little
qualcosa	something/anything
qualcuno	someone/somebody
tanti, tante	so much, so many
tanto... quanto, tanta... quanta	as/so much . . . as
tanti... quanti, tante... quante	as many . . . as
troppo, troppa	too much
troppi, troppe	too many
tutti e due, tutte e due	both
tutti, tutte	(all) everyone
tutto, tutta	everything
uno, una	one

Preposizioni semplici

Here follows a list of verbs and the **preposizioni semplici** that usually introduce a noun or a verb. *Phrasal verbs are in italics.*

Preposizioni Semplici

di

accettare di fare	to agree to doing
accontentarsi di qualcosa/di fare	to make do, to be content with
accusare qualcuno di qualcosa/di fare	to accuse someone of something/of doing
avere intenzione di fare	to have the intention of doing
consistere di qualcosa/in qualcosa	to be made of something; to consist of something
credere di fare	to believe that one is doing
discutere di qualcosa	to discuss something
essere partecipe di qualcosa	to be sharing something
essere sicuro di qualcuno, qualcosa/di fare	to be certain of/to
fare parte di qualcosa	to take part in something
parlare di qualcuno, qualcosa/di fare	to talk about someone, something
pensare di fare	to think of
ridere di qualcuno, qualcosa	to laugh about someone/something
rifiutarsi di fare	to refuse to do
sentirsi di fare	to feel up to, to feel like
soffrire di	to suffer from
sforzarsi di fare	to make an effort; to try one's best
sognare di fare	to dream of doing

a

abituarsi a qualcuno/qualcosa, a fare	to get used to someone/something, to doing
acconsentire a fare	to agree to doing
aiutare a fare	to help to
appartenere a qualcuno/qualcosa	to belong to someone/something
arrivare a/in un posto	to arrive in/at a place
assistere a qualcosa	to attend something
assomigliare a qualcuno	to resemble/look like someone
aversene a male	to take offense

domandare (qualcosa) a qualcuno	to ask something from someone/to ask someone
cavarsela a fare	to manage to do
chiedere (qualcosa) a qualcuno	to ask someone for something
cominciare/incominciare a fare	to start to do/doing
continuare a fare	to go on/keep on/carry on with doing
contribuire a qualcosa, a fare	to contribute to something/to doing
costringere a fare	to force to do
credere a qualcuno/qualcosa	to believe someone/something
darle a qualcuno	to beat someone up
decidersi a fare	to make up one's mind to do
dire arrivederci/addio a qualcuno	to say/bid good-bye/farewell to someone
essere abituato a qualcuno/qualcosa, a fare	to be used to someone/something, to doing
essere bravo a qualcosa/a fare (and **non essere bravo a**)	to be good at something, at doing
essere d'accordo con qualcuno/a fare	to agree with someone/to doing
essere gentile con qualcuno	to be kind/polite to someone
fare bene/male a fare	to do the right/wrong thing in doing
farne parte a qualcuno	to bring someone into the loop; to share something with someone
indurre a fare	to induce to do
insegnare a fare	to teach how to do
insistere su qualcosa, a fare	to insist on something/on doing
invitare a qualcosa, a fare	to invite to something, to do
imparare a fare	to learn to
mettersi a fare	to start to do/doing, to set out to
obbligare a fare	to oblige/force to
ostinarsi a fare	to persist in doing something
pensare a qualcuno/qualcosa	to think of someone/something
persuadere a fare	to persuade to do
provare a fare	to try to do
riuscire a/essere riuscito a fare	to be able to do; to have succeeded in doing
rinunciare a qualcuno/qualcosa, a fare	to give up someone/something, doing
rispondere a qualcuno	to answer someone
sbagliare a fare	to make a mistake in doing
sorridere a qualcuno	to smile at someone
spiegare (qualcosa) a qualcuno	to explain (something) to someone

da

dipendere da qualcuno/qualcosa	to depend on someone/something
essere colpito da qualcuno qualcosa;	to be hit by something; to be struck by
essere colpito da qualcuno qualcosa	someone/something
essere deluso da qualcuno/qualcosa	to be disappointed with someone/something
fare da	to act as; to play the role of
partecipare a qualcosa	to participate in something
prendere da qualcuno	to take after someone
uscire da (un posto)	to get out of/to exit from

in

credere in qualcuno/qualcosa	to believe in someone/something
entrare in (un posto)/entrare in argomento	to enter (a place)/to address an issue

su

affacciarsi su	to face; to be facing
contare su qualcuno/qualcosa	to count on someone/something
essere d'accordo su qualcosa	to agree about/on something
scusarsi con qualcuno	to apologize to someone
tirare su qualcuno/qualcosa	to lift someone's spirits; to raise children; to pull up someone/something; to build up something quickly
tirarsi su	to recover; to cheer oneself up

con

avercela con qualcuno	to be angry/cross with someone
combattere/lottare con qualcuno	to fight with someone
congratularsi con qualcuno	to congratulate someone
discutere con qualcuno	to discuss with someone
essere adirato/arrabbiato con qualcuno	to be angry/cross with someone
essere d'accordo con qualcuno	to agree with someone
prendersela con qualcuno	to have it in for someone
scusarsi con qualcuno	to apologize to someone
uscire con; uscire con qualcuno	to go out with; to date someone

per

combattere/lottare per qualcosa	to fight over something
congratularsi per qualcosa	to congratulate (someone) for/on
essere adirato/arrabbiato per qualcosa	to be angry/cross for something
essere deluso per qualcosa	to be disappointed with/at/about something
essere responsabile per qualcuno/qualcosa	to be responsible for someone/something; to be in charge of something
essere spiacente per qualcuno/qualcosa	to be sorry for someone, for/about something
finire per fare	to end up by doing
prendersela per qualcosa	to get upset about something
scusarsi per qualcosa	to apologize for something
stare per fare	to be about to do

tra/fra

dividere qualcosa tra	to divide something between/among
dividersi/separarsi da qualcuno	to separate from someone
dividersi tra	to divide oneself between

Prepositions and Complements

Here follow tables of the **preposizioni semplici** and some of the most important **complementi** they can introduce, accompanied by examples.

Preposizione Semplici, Complementi, and Examples

di (of, about)

Complement	Complementi	Example
Specification	**Specificazione**	L'amico **di Stefano** è arrivato.
Material	**Materia**	Vorrei un abito **di lino**.
Means	**Mezzo**	Si nutrono **di bacche**.
Manner	**Modo**	Vanno **di fretta**.
Denomination	**Denominazione**	Abbiamo visitato l'isola **di Rodi**.
Partitive	**Partitivo**	**Di tutti i miei amici**, il più fortunato è Giorgio.
Cause	**Causa**	Crollo **di sonno**.
Subject matter	**Argomento**	Parliamo **di vacanze**.
Age	**Età**	Silvia ha un bambino **di tre anni**.
Lack	**Privazione**	La capanna era priva **di bagni**.
Abundance	**Abbondanza**	Il lago è pieno **di pesci**.
Comparison	**Paragone**	Mio fratello è più buono **di te**.
Time when	**Tempo determinato**	Vittorio lavora **di notte**.
Quantity	**Quantità**	Affittano un campo **di cento acri**.
Motion from	**Moto da luogo**	Usciamo **di casa**.
Motion through	**Moto per luogo**	Passarono **di là**.
Origin	**Origine**	Siete **di Venezia**?
Limitation	**Limitazione**	Lei è una persona buona **di carattere**.
Quality	**Qualità**	È una donna **di grande ingegno**.

a (to, at, in)

Complement	Complementi	Example
End	**Termine**	Porta i fiori **a tua sorella**.
Means	**Mezzo**	Gli esploratori fecero il viaggio **a cavallo**.
Manner	**Modo**	Parlano **a bassa voce**.
Purpose	**Fine**	Carlo lavora **alla costruzione** del ponte.
Time when	**Tempo determinato**	**A settembre** si vendemmia.
Place where	**Stato in luogo**	Resto **a Genova**.
Motion toward	**Moto a luogo**	Andrò **a Genova**.
Age	**Età**	**A tre anni** suonava il piano.
Price	**Prezzo**	Le arance si vendono **a 5 euro al chilo**.
Limitation	**Limitazione**	Nessuno lo batte **a poker**.
Quality	**Qualità**	Vuoi una tovaglia **a fiori**?

da (from, by, since)

Complement	Complementi	Example
Motion toward	**Moto a luogo**	Verrò **da voi**.
Motion from	**Moto da luogo**	Lui arriva **da Arezzo**.
Place where	**Stato in luogo**	Staranno **da Carla**.
Motion through	**Moto per luogo**	Mio padre è passato **da Bologna**.

Duration of time	**Tempo continuato**	Piove **da due giorni.**
Cause	**Causa**	Riccardo svenne **dalla paura.**
Agent	**Agente**	Sei stato interrogato **dalla polizia?**
Limitation	**Limitazione**	Ci vedo male **da un occhio.**
Origin	**Origine**	Il suo fidanzato discende **da un'illustre dinastia.**
Qualità	**Qualità**	È una macchina **dalle linee eleganti.**
Purpose	**Fine**	Abbiamo bisogno di una borsa **da mare.**
Separation	**Separazione**	Allontaniamoci **dal bar.**

in (in, at)

Complement	Complementi	Example
Place where	**Stato in luogo**	Irene abita **in campagna.**
Motion toward	**Moto a luogo**	Vado **in spiaggia.**
Material	**Materia**	Il pavimento è **in marmo,** non **in legno.**
Purpose	**Fine**	Il soprano canterà **in suo onore.**
Means	**Mezzo**	Facciamo un giro **in bici.**
Duration of time	**Tempo continuato**	Stefano ha risolto quel problema **in un'ora.**
Time when	**Tempo determinato**	Passo a trovarti **in serata.**
Manner	**Modo**	Lavorate **in gruppo.**
Limitation	**Limitazione**	Mario batte tutti **in velocità.**

con (with)

Complement	Complementi	Example
Company	**Compagnia**	L'ho vista **con sua zia.**
Union	**Unione**	Mi piacciono le fragole **con la panna.**
Means	**Mezzo**	Elisabetta esce **con la macchina** di suo padre.
Manner	**Modo**	Quel signore saluta sempre **con grande gentilezza.**
Cause	**Causa**	**Col gelo** le piante sono morte.
Time when	**Tempo determinato**	**Con l'inverno** arriva la neve.
Quality	**Qualità**	Hai un cane **col pelo marrone?**
Material	**Materia**	L'ha fatto **con dei vecchi copertoni.**

su (on, about)

Complement	Complementi	Example
Subject matter	**Argomento**	Fa una conferenza **sulla guerra in Iraq.**
Place where	**Stato in luogo**	Dormono **sul terrazzo.**
Motion toward	**Moto a luogo**	Si arrampicano **sull'albero.**
Manner	**Modo**	Ci siamo accordati **sulla parola.**
Distributive	**Distributivo**	Nicola ha risposto a due domande **su tre.**
Age	**Età**	Suo padre è **sui sessant'anni.**

per (for, through)

Complement	Complementi	Example
Duration of time	**Tempo continuato**	C'è stato il sole **per tre giorni.**
Purpose	**Fine**	Studio **per l'esame.**
Cause	**Causa**	Non è andato in vacanza **per motivi** di salute.
Motion toward	**Moto a luogo**	Partiamo **per il mare?**
Motion through	**Moto per luogo**	Passiamo **per il bosco.**

Quantity	**Quantità**	Il bosco si estendeva **per tre chilometri**.
Limitation	**Limitazione**	**Per generosità** Barbara batte tutti.
Price	**Prezzo**	Ho avuto la macchina **per cinquemila euro**.

fra/tra (**in, between, among, through, etc.**)

Complement	Complementi	Example
Time when	**Tempo determinato**	La mamma tornerà **fra** un'ora.
Place where	**Stato in luogo**	Ho perso la pallina da golf **tra i cespugli**.
Motion through	**Moto per luogo**	Passeggiavano **tra gli alberi**.
Partitive	**Partitivo**	**Tra tutte** la più bella è Giulia.

Answer Key

Unit 1

1-1

1. c	3. a	5. d
2. f	4. e	6. b

1-2

1. e	3. f	5. c
2. d	4. a	6. b

1-3

1. f	3. a	5. i	7. e	9. b
2. d	4. g	6. c	8. j	10. h

1-4

1. Io rido.	3. Loro sciano.	5. Lui studia.	7. Lei vede.	9. Noi capiamo.
2. Noi paghiamo.	4. Tu corri.	6. Lui abbaia.	8. Voi sentite.	10. Essi mangiano il miele.

1-5

1. Lui sogna molto ogni notte.
2. «Alberto, hai visto il mio libro»?
3. I miei zii viaggiano molto.
4. Lei adora il cinema.
5. «Voi sapete un mucchio di cose»!
6. Noi capiamo il tedesco.
7. Ma loro dove vanno?
8. Il gatto? Lui gioca sempre con il mio maglione.
9. «Tu fai troppi regali ai bambini».
10. Loro vogliono entrare?

1-6

1. Noi e voi guardiamo il film.
2. Tu e lui giocate sempre a scacchi.
3. Tu ed io partiamo domani.
4. Noi e loro compriamo la ditta.
5. Lui e lei stanno insieme da anni.
6. Voi e loro non parlate abbastanza.

1-7

1. Lei è una brava ballerina.
2. Lui è andato a Londra.
3. «Signor Rossi, Lei è andato a Londra»?
4. «Signore, Lei ha bisogno di qualcosa»?
5. «Signora, Lei desidera un antipasto»?
6. «Voi partirete con l'autobus delle otto».
7. Lui ha sognato suo padre.
8. «Passi prima Lei, Signora Maffei».
9. «Signore e Signori, Loro siano i benvenuti».
10. «Voi avete visto quel film»?

1-8

1. d	4. b	7. e
2. h	5. g	8. a
3. i	6. c	9. f

1-9

1. It's better to go home.
2. "Who is knocking at the door?" "It's your sister."
3. "What day is today?" "It's Thursday."
4. You bought everything, didn't you?
5. It's beginning to snow.
6. It's important that he hears your version.
7. It's my doctor who recommended that specialist.
8. It's worthwhile talking to her.

1-10
1. Tu non porti a spasso il cane.
2. Noi non andiamo a camminare in montagna d'inverno.
3. Lei non ama il sushi.
4. Loro non telefonano alla zia.
5. Voi non guardate il calcio alla televisione?
6. Lui non porta il gatto dal veterinario?
7. Io non parto sabato per l'Argentina.
8. Noi non affittiamo la casa al mare.

1-11
1. b
2. d
3. f
4. a
5. c
6. e

1-12
1. Noi non andiamo a Roma, ma voi sì.
2. Io uso il telefonino, lei no.
3. Loro non vogliono un cane, ma io sì.
4. Lui ruggisce; lei miagola.
5. Loro non vogliono il gelato; tu sì?
6. Lei guadagna molti soldi, lui no.
7. Lui ha risposto, lei no.
8. Lui abbaia quando è solo, ma lei no.

Unit 2

2-1
1. Lo cercano.
2. Lo guardate?
3. Giovanni li porta al mare.
4. La batto sempre a scacchi.
5. Lo chiami?
6. Le raccolgono.
7. La mangi?
8. Li nutre.
9. Le porti in casa?
10. Le aiutano.

2-2
1. Cercano lui.
2. —
3. Giovanni porta loro al mare.
4. Batto sempre lei a scacchi.
5. Chiami lui?
6. —
7. —
8. Nutre loro.
9. —
10. Aiutano loro.

2-3
1. Ti chiama?
2. La contatto presto, Signor Vanzetti.
3. Vi conosco bene, ragazzi.
4. Vi invitiamo a cena.
5. Ti chiamo ogni giorno.
6. La vedo al bar, Signora.
7. Vi portiamo all'aeroporto, Signori.

2-4
Pietro: «*Mi* chiamavi»?
Giulia: «Sì, *ti* chiamavo. Ho bisogno di un favore. *Mi* porti in montagna»?
Pietro: «Non *ti* porto in montagna, perché devo andare a Milano. Quando torno, vuoi andare a cena da mia sorella»?
Giulia: «Preferirei di no. Quando *ti* trovo in casa da solo»?
Pietro: «*Mi* trovi domani sera. Vieni, così facciamo due chiacchiere in pace».

2-5
Pietro: «Chiamavi *me* o lui»?
Giulia: «Chiamavo *te*. Ho bisogno di un favore. Domani, porti *me* ed i miei amici in montagna»?
Pietro: «Non porto *te* ed i tuoi amici in montagna, perché devo andare a Milano. Quando torno, vuoi andare a cena da mia sorella»?
Giulia: «Preferirei di no. Quando trovo *te* da solo»?
Pietro: «Trovi *me* da solo domani sera. Vieni, così facciamo due chiacchiere in pace».

2-6
1. Lo compro. / Non lo compro.
2. Li avvisa. / Non li avvisa.
3. La pulisco. / Non la pulisco.
4. Le guardiamo. / Non le guardiamo.
5. La ama molto. / Non la ama molto.
6. La rileggono. / Non la rileggono.
7. Lo approva. / Non lo approva.
8. Li invitiamo a pranzo. / Non li invitiamo a pranzo.
9. La portiamo al mare. / Non la portiamo al mare.

2-7

1. —
2. Avvisa loro. / Non avvisa loro.
3. —
4. —
5. —

6. Rileggono lei. / Non rileggono lei.
7. Approva lui. / Non approva lui.
8. Invitiamo loro a pranzo. / Non invitiamo loro a pranzo.
9. Portiamo lei al mare. / Non portiamo lei al mare.

2-8

1. Pensi di aiutarlo?
2. Ha deciso di assumerla?
3. Sei sicura di batterlo a dama?
4. Vi siete ricordati di salutarli?

5. Credono di aiutarci.
6. Ho i soldi per pagarvi.
7. Vengono a trovarmi.
8. È contento di vederti.

2-9

1. Portale in casa!
2. Non mangiarloe tutto!
3. Aiutatela!
4. Non compratela.

5. Portalo, mi raccomando.
6. Salutala da parte mia!
7. Non seguitelo!
8. Invitali a cena!

2-10

1. Giovanna sta avvertendolo.
2. Stiamo chiamandovi.
3. Stanno pagandoci.
4. Mia sorella sta ringraziandoti.

5. State aiutandoli?
6. I miei amici stanno seguendola.
7. Sta osservandomi.

2-11

1. L(o)'ho comprato. / Non l(o)'ho comprato.
2. Li ha avvisati. / Non li avvisati.
3. L(o)'ho pulita. / Non l(o)'ho pulita.
4. Le abbiamo guardate. / Non le abbiamo guardate.
5. L(a)'ha vista. / Non l(a)'ha vista.
6. L(a)'hanno rieletta. / Non l(a)'hanno rieletta.
7. Li abbiamo invitati a pranzo. / Non li abbiamo invitati a pranzo.
8. L(a)'hanno portata al mare. / Non l(a)'hanno portata al mare.

2-12

1. Li possiamo servire. / Possiamo servirli.
2. La vuoi aiutare? / Vuoi aiutarla?
3. Lo devono invitare. / Devono invitarlo.
4. Lo vogliamo pagare? / Vogliamo pagarlo?

5. La sa scrivere. / Sa scriverla.
6. La devo guardare. / Devo guardarla.
7. La potete aprire. / Potete aprirla.
8. Lo sanno riparare. / Sanno ripararlo.

2-13

1. Volevi un vestito nuovo. Hai potuto comprarlo?
2. Non dovevi pagarli. Non hanno finito il lavoro.
3. Mi domandi se voglio invitare anche lui? Assolutamente no!
4. Gli organizzatori hanno assegnato i nostri compagni di tennis. Non volevo certo lei.
5. Abbiamo preso un mucchio di granchi. Li possono mangiare?
6. Ama molto sua sorella. Vuole aiutarla il più possibile.
7. Devono convincerli a venire.

2-14

1. Pietro ha osato rimproverarla.
2. Clara sembra capirmi.
3. Noi li abbiamo lasciati partire.
4. Voi mi fate mangiare troppe caramelle.

5. Loro preferiscono contattarti direttamente.
6. Ti lascio comprare quel vestito.
7. Tu l(a)'hai fatta piangere.
8. Lui mi ha lasciato piangere.

2-15

1. «Vorrei tanto aiutarti, ma non ho un soldo». «Lo capisco».
2. «La nostra squadra vincerà sicuramente». «Chi lo dice»?
3. Si crede intelligente, ma non lo è.
4. Vuole tornare; non l(o)'ha detto, ma l(o)'ho capito.
5. Ha giocato solo con Lucia. L(o)'hai notato?
6. Volevi andare in montagna. L(o)'hai poi fatto?
7. «Hanno divorziato». «L(o)'ho saputo».

2-16

1. Ci sono troppi libri sullo scaffale.
2. Possono vederci dalla strada.
3. Ci vado domani.
4. C'era una volta un drago gentile...
5. Ci siete, se passo stasera?
6. Ci ha pensato molto, ma ha rifiutato.
7. C'è molto pane a casa.

Unit 3

3-1

1. She writes long letters to him.
2. We offered a ride to you.
3. I sent a package to you.
4. They bought a car for her.
5. He gave a suggestion to them.
6. You sold her jewelry to them.
7. Do a favor for me.

3-2

1. Compriamo un regalo per voi.
2. Scrivi a lei?
3. Offrono aiuto a noi?
4. Parla a te?
5. Do a lui un consiglio.
6. Telefonate a loro?
7. Manda un pacco a me.

3-3

1. Abbiamo detto loro arrivederci.
2. Ha affidato a lui i suoi investimenti.
3. Ha raccontato a me la fine il film!
4. Avete promesso a lei di non dire più le bugie!
5. Ha detto loro la sua versione dell'incidente.

3-4

1. Vi compriamo un gelato.
2. Gli raccontano una storia.
3. Le mando dei fiori.
4. Ci offre il suo aiuto.
5. Gli compro un televisore.
6. Mi scrivi una cartolina?
7. Ti regalo il mio orologio.

3-5

1. Gli vuole bene?
2. Gli dico tutto.
3. Perché non gli racconti la tua storia?
4. Gli regaliamo un televisione nuova.
5. Vi prometto un servizio migliore la prossima volta.
6. Il suo amante le compra dei gioielli carissimi.

3-6

1. Gli abbiamo detto arrivederci.
2. Gli ha affidato i suoi investimenti.
3. Mi ha raccontato la fine del film!
4. Le avete promesso di non dire più le bugie!
5. Gli ha detto la sua versione dell'incidente.

3-7

1. Pensi di telefonargli?
2. Ha deciso di offrirle il lavoro?
3. Hai tempo di spiegarci quel problema?
4. Hanno deciso di darvi le informazioni.
5. Pensano di parlarti delle vacanze.
6. Sai scriverle un bel biglietto di auguri?
7. Crede di farmi un favore?

3-8
1. Parlagli del problema con i vicini!
2. Non dirmi che sei stanca!
3. Raccontateci i vostri progetti!
4. Non consegnatele il pacco!
5. Non offrirle la cena!

3-9
1. Le ho scritto una lettera.
2. Gli sta telefonando.
3. Vi abbiamo fatto un regalo.
4. Ci hanno offerto un passaggio.
5. Stai mandandomi un e-mail?
6. Sto comprandoti un libro.

3-10
1. Posso parlarLe, Signora?
2. Posso presentarLe mia moglie, Signore?
3. Vorrei offrirti una cena.
4. Vogliono parlarci di un progetto.
5. Dovete consegnarmi un pacco?
6. Possiamo offrirvi qualcosa da bere, Signori?
7. Devi confessargli il tuo errore.

3-11
1. Desiderate darle un suggerimento?
2. Mi lascia mangiare la sua fetta di torta.
3. Hanno osato parlargli.
4. Ci ha fatto mandare un regalo.
5. Non gli abbiamo lasciato finire il discorso.
6. Sembra credergli.
7. Preferisci comprarle un CD?
8. Non gli lascia usare la sua automobile.

3-12
1. Ice cream is pleasing to us.
2. Books are pleasing to her.
3. That dog is pleasing to you.
4. Cats are not pleasing to them.
5. Anna is pleasing to you.
6. Movies are pleasing to him.
7. The tango is pleasing to me.

3-13
1. Ti piace il cinema?
2. Non gli piace la carne.
3. Non ci piace il Primo Ministro.
4. Non mi piacciono quei libri.
5. Non gli piace la nuova casa.
6. Le piacciono i tuoi fratelli.
7. Mi piace il jazz.
8. Non ti piace il jazz.

3-14
1. A loro è piaciuta l'opera?
2. A voi non vi è piaciuto quel ristorante.
3. A lui non gli è piaciuta la minestra.
4. A lei è piaciuto il viaggio.
5. A te sono piaciuti i loro CD?
6. A lei piacciono i tuoi fratelli.
7. A me piace il jazz, a te no.
8. A noi è piaciuto il film, a voi no.

Unit 4

4-1
1. I'm giving it to her.
2. She's writing it to him.
3. We're opening it for him.
4. You are sending it to them.
5. I'm preparing it for you.
6. You are closing it for me.
7. They're cleaning it for her.
8. He's showing them to us.
9. She's delivering them to you.

4-2
1. Glielo do.
2. Gliela scrive.
3. Gliela apriamo.
4. Glielo mandate.
5. Te lo preparo.
6. Me lo chiudi.
7. Gliela puliscono.
8. Ce li mostra.
9. Ve li consegna.

4-3
1. I'm building it for them.
2. He doesn't mail it to me.
3. Will they open it for you?
4. You're offering it to him.
5. I will give it to her.
6. He's preparing it for them.
7. You're preparing it for us.
8. They will explain it to you.

4-4

1. Mandaglielo!
2. Imprestagliela!
3. Portatecelo!
4. Offriteglielo!
5. Mostramele!

4-5

1. Hai detto a Luigi di portargliele?
2. Dandomela, mi hai aiutato molto.
3. Rendiglielo!
4. Pensano di mandarglieli?
5. Comprandoceli, ci avete fatto un bel regalo.

4-6

1. Non mandarglielo!
2. Non prestargliela!
3. Non portatecelo!
4. Non offriteglielo!
5. Non mostrarmele!

4-7

1. Gliela stai dando.
2. Glielo stiamo portando.
3. Ve la stanno preparando.
4. Glielo state mostrando.
5. Te la sto costruendo.
6. Gliela stiamo indicando.
7. Me la sta pitturando.

4-8

1. Gliel(o)'ho costruito.
2. Me l'ha spedita.
3. Te l(o)'hanno aperto.
4. Me l(o)'hai offerto.
5. Glielo sto dando.
6. Gliele ha scritte.
7. Ce lo state preparando.
8. Ve l(o)'hanno spiegato.

4-9

1. Voglio ricordarglielo.
2. Devi raccontargliela.
3. Sanno mandarglieli.
4. Può comprartelo.
5. Volete promettergliela?
6. Devo vendervelo.
7. Vuole aprirmela.

4-10

1. Glielo voglio ricordare.
2. Gliela devi raccontare.
3. Glieli sanno mandare.
4. Te lo può comprare.
5. Gliela volete promettere?
6. Ve lo devo vendere.
7. Me la vuole aprire.

4-11

1. Voglio organizzarglielo.
2. Sanno aprircela.
3. Puoi affittarglielo.
4. Dobbiamo venderteli.
5. Vogliamo comprargliela.
6. So chiuderglielo.
7. Devi scaricarcelo.
8. Deve pagarglielo.
9. Vuole offrircelo.
10. Sa dargliela.

4-12

1. Vorresti averglielo organizzato?
2. Possono averglielo affittato.
3. Vorreste avermeli venduti?
4. Dovrebbero averglielo finito.
5. Devono avervelo scaricato.

4-13
1. Faglielo finire!
2. Ce lo lasciate portare?
3. Non ve la lasciano invitare.
4. Fateglielo portare.

5. Gliela lasci vedere?
6. Me lo lasciate vedere?
7. Te la lasciano prendere a prestito.

Unit 5

5-1
1. Si pesa ogni giorno.
2. Si rade due volte al giorno.
3. Vi truccate per lo spettacolo.
4. Si spogliano. / Si svestono.
5. La gatta si lava.

6. Mia madre si spazzola i capelli ogni sera.
7. Mi copro quando fa freddo.
8. Ti vesti?
9. Ci svestiamo. / Ci spogliamo.

5-2
1. Pettinati!
2. Devo cambiarmi.
3. Le dico di lavarsi.
4. Copritevi!

5. Non pesarti di nuovo!
6. Può asciugarsi?
7. Devono pulirsi.

5-3
1. Si è pesata una settimana fa.
2. Quando si è rasato?
3. Si sono truccati per lo spettacolo.
4. Vi siete svestiti.

5. La gatta si è lavata.
6. Mi sono coperto bene.
7. Perché ti sei scoperto?

5-4
1. Le piace spazzolarsi i capelli.
2. Pulisciti la faccia!
3. Si pettina i capelli, ma non si fa la barba.
4. Abbiamo dovuto cambiarci le calze dopo la partita.

5. Si truccano il viso.
6. Ti fai la barba? / Ti radi?
7. Ci copriamo la testa in chiesa.

5-5
1. Mi compro un abito da sera lungo.
2. Volete cucinarvi un arrosto?
3. Non bevetevi tutta la bottiglia!
4. Elena ha intenzione di giocarsi 1.000.000,00 euro alla roulette.

5. Mio marito si stira le camicie.
6. Ci prepariamo le valigie.
7. Si vendono tutte le azioni.

5-6
1. I bambini non si sono puliti le unghie.
2. Mia nonna non si è pettinata bene i capelli.
3. Vi siete coperti la testa?
4. Nicola si è cambiato i pantaloni.
5. Mi sono messa le calze.

6. Si tolga pure il cappotto, Signora.
7. Le mie sorelle si sono truccate solo gli occhi.
8. Gli attori si sono truccati tutto il viso.
9. Il nonno si è fatto la barba?
10. Ci siamo lavati le mani.

5-7
1. Franca e Nicoletta si vogliono bene.
2. Massimo e Luciana si sposano.
3. Ci telefoniamo domani?
4. I miei fratelli si aiutano molto.

5. Ci capiamo.
6. Olga ed io ci scriviamo.
7. Si vedono domani.
8. Si sono separati dopo vent'anni di matrimonio.

5-8
1. Franca e Nicoletta si sono sempre volute bene.
2. Massimo e Luciana si sono sposati un anno fa.
3. Ci siamo scambiati i numeri di telefono.
4. I miei fratelli si sono sempre aiutati molto.
5. Non ci siamo mai capiti.

6. Olga ed io ci siamo scritte lunghe lettere per molti anni.
7. Si sono visti una settimana fa.
8. Si sono abbracciati.

5-9
1. Me li cambio.
2. Se li gioca alla roulette.
3. Te li trucchi?
4. Se le mettono?
5. Ve lo comprate?

5-10
1. Te le sei preparate?
2. Se lo sono tolto.
3. Devono essersele lucidate.
4. Ce lo siamo coperto.
5. Ve le siete asciugate?
6. Se lo è cambiato.
7. Me lo sono tolto.
8. Se la è cucinata.

5-11
1. People believe that there will be another terrorist attack.
2. Guys, we are leaving at six tomorrow morning.
3. One learns more quickly when one is young.
4. Rumor has it (people say) that the prince will marry a foreigner. We'll see.
5. One eats well in that restaurant. / They serve good food in that restaurant.
6. We talked a lot about selling the firm.
7. We (People) work too much nowadays.
8. Shall we play golf on Sunday?

5-12
1. Si dà troppo poco aiuto economico ai paesi poveri.
2. Si crede troppo ai mass media.
3. Non si crede ai politici.
4. Si muore di fame!
5. Si pensa di vendere la casa.
6. Si dice che lui voglia diventare presidente.
7. Si può giocare a poker in quel club.
8. Non si vuole scommettere sulla borsa adesso.

Unit 6

6-1
1. Ne ho sentito parlare.
2. Ne sai qualcosa?
3. Ne apprezzo il senso dell'umorismo.
4. Ne conoscete i genitori?
5. Ne è rimasto colpito.
6. Ne ricordi il nome?
7. Ne è la baby-sitter.
8. Ne abbiamo una buona opinione.

6-2
1. Ne ho parlato a mio padre.
2. Non ne sapeva niente.
3. Ne abbiamo una pessima opinione.
4. Non ne vedono la necessità.
5. Ne vale la pena?
6. Non riuscite a farne a meno?

6-3
1. a little/some
2. of the
3. a little/some
4. of the
5. a little/some
6. a little/some
7. of the

6-4
1. Ne bevo.
2. Ne rivedranno tre a Natale.
3. Ne compriamo.
4. Ne vendono una.
5. Ne vogliono noleggiare uno.
6. Ne prendete uno?
7. Speditene una a vostra zia!
8. Coglietene dieci.
9. Ne vogliono regalare mille alla biblioteca pubblica.
10. Non ne mette nel caffè.

6-5

1. «Avete comprato degli zucchini»? «Sì, ne abbiamo comprati».
2. «Hanno preso dei panini»? «Sì, ne hanno presi cinque».
3. «Hai mangiato dei cioccolatini»? «Sì, ne ho mangiato uno».
4. «Hai mangiato delle pesche»? «Sì, ne ho mangiata una».
5. «Avete bevuto abbastanza acqua»? «Sì, ne abbiamo bevuta abbastanza».
6. «Ha trovato delle ricette interessanti»? «Sì, ne ha trovate tre».
7. «Hai visto dei bei film»? «No, non ne ho visto nessuno».
8. «Hai visto delle belle gonne»? «No, non ne ho vista nessuna».

6-6

1. Gliene ho portato.
2. Gliene abbiamo comprato.
3. Ce ne hai comprato?
4. Gliene avete vendute?
5. Non te ne ha mandato nessuno?
6. Devono avergliene imprestata una.
7. Te ne ho presi.
8. Volete comprarmene una?

6-7

1. Gliene abbiamo parlato.
2. Me ne ha parlato.
3. Gliene ho riferito.
4. Ce ne hanno dato buone informazioni.

6-8

1. Me ne cucino uno.
2. Se ne comprano una parte.
3. Se ne trucca solo uno?
4. Te ne prepari una?
5. Ve ne bevete tre?
6. Se ne cinque!

6-9

1. Te ne sei innamorato?
2. Ce ne interessiamo.
3. Ve ne siete dimenticati?
4. Se ne sono liberati.
5. La mia amica se ne è vergognata.
6. Dario se ne è stancato.
7. Me ne sono stancata.
8. Ve ne siete pentiti?
9. Non se ne interessa piú.

Unit 7

7-1

1. Gioco a carte con voi.
2. Da lei non abbiamo ricevuto niente.
3. Ho affidato tutti i miei affari a lui.
4. Si fida totalmente di lei.
5. Tra loro ci sono sempre discussioni.
6. Passiamo da lei?
7. Quella fotografia è stata presa da lui.
8. Scrivo un libro su di lei.

7-2

1. Parla con loro ogni giorno.
2. Olga non lavora per lui.
3. Vai da lei?
4. Vive sopra di me.
5. Deve scegliere tra te e me.
6. La cena è stata preparata da lui.
7. Contiamo su di te.

Unit 8

8-1

1. Chi è lei?
2. Chi non vuole il caffé?
3. Chi sono loro?
4. Chi sei tu?
5. Chi parla tedesco?
6. Chi siete voi?
7. Chi sono io?
8. Chi è il tuo amico/la tua amica?

8-2

1. Who is coming to the party?
2. Who is buying bread?
3. Who is that girl?
4. Who are they?
5. Who catches mice?
6. Who sold the castle?
7. Who sold it?

8-3
1. Chi parte?
2. Chi ha aperto la porta?
3. Chi deve pagare il conto?
4. Chi vende la macchina?
5. Chi vuole il dessert?
6. Chi va al cinema?
7. Chi non mangia carne?

8-4
1. Chi l'ha bevuto?
2. Chi si è sbagliato?
3. Chi le ha scelte?
4. Chi l'ha vista?
5. Chi si è laureato degli iscritti a Lettere?
6. Chi li ha controllati?
7. Chi l'ha rotto?
8. Chi l'ha rotta?

8-5
1. Chi chiami?
2. Chi assume?
3. Chi ama?
4. Chi contattano?
5. Chi conoscete?
6. Chi paghiamo per primi?
7. Chi devo chiamare?

8-6
1. Whom did you see at the stadium?
2. Whom do we want to invite?
3. Whom did your sister marry?
4. Whom did you call for that job?
5. Whom did they interview on the radio?
6. Whom did I hire as consultant?

8-7
1. Chi hai chiamato?
2. Chi ha assunto Nadia?
3. Chi ha amato tutta la vita?
4. Chi hanno contattato?
5. Chi avete visto?
6. Chi hai incontrato?
7. Chi abbiamo pagato per primo?

8-8
1. Di chi è questa valigia?
2. Di chi sono quei gatti?
3. Di chi sono questi fiori?
4. Di chi è quell'automobile?

8-9
1. Whose sister is that girl?
2. Whose fiancé was your cousin? (To whom was your cousin engaged?)
3. Whose child is Giovanni?
4. Whose brothers are Marcello and Piero?
5. Whose friends are those boys?

8-10
1. Di chi è la macchina che si è rotta?
2. Di chi è il gatto che si è perso?
3. Di chi sono i CD che hai copiato?
4. Di chi è il portafoglio che il ladro ha rubato?
5. Di chi è la moto che stanno guidando?
6. Di chi è il dipinto che stiamo comprando?
7. Di chi sono i fiori che stiamo raccogliendo?
8. Di chi sono i pacchi che stiamo spedendo?

8-11
1. Con chi vive?
2. Per chi lavorano?
3. Da chi sono consegnati quei fiori?
4. A chi ha parlato?
5. Per chi comprano un computer?
6. A chi appartengono queste scarpe?

8-12
1. A chi ha portato la cena?
2. A chi hai dedicato il libro?
3. Con chi andate in vacanza?
4. Da chi è stato dipinto *L'urlo*?
5. Con chi fa il prossimo film?
6. Su chi posso contare?
7. A chi dobbiamo consegnarlo?

8-13

1. Che cosa vuole?
2. Che cosa mangiano?
3. Che cosa succede in piazza?
4. Che cosa pensate di fare?
5. Che cosa diciamo ai nostri genitori?
6. Che cosa compri?

8-14

1. A che cosa pensi?
2. Di che cosa si lamentano?
3. Di che cosa si preoccupa?
4. Non so che fare.
5. Domandagli che cosa vuol fare.
6. Non ricordo che cosa stavo dicendo.

8-15

1. Hai visto molte biciclette. Quale hai comprato?
2. Dobbiamo scegliere un medico. Qual è meglio?
3. Ha buttato via molti vestiti. Quali ha tenuto?
4. Puoi avere tre giocattoli. Quali vuoi?
5. Hanno fatto molte critiche al nostro progetto. Qual era la più seria?
6. Qual è il tuo cappotto?
7. Qual è il loro numero di telefono?

8-16

1. Che (cosa) fai domani?
2. Ci sono molti libri. Vorrei sapere quale preferisci.
3. A (che) cosa stanno giocando?
4. Dovete raccontare alla polizia (che) cosa vi è successo.
5. Ha guardato molte riviste. A quale ha fatto abbonamento?
6. Che (cosa) le hai detto per farla piangere?
7. Quale dei suoi amici ti è più simpatico?

8-17

1. «Quanto costa quella borsa»?
2. «Siamo andati tutti in barca». «Quanti eravate»?
3. «Siamo andate tutte in barca». «Quante eravate»?
4. «Ho visto tantissimi uccelli, non so quanti».
5. «Starò via alcuni giorni». «Sai dirmi esattamente quanti»?
6. «Abbiamo invitato cento persone». «Non so quante accetteranno».
7. «Quanto conta il suo appoggio»?
8. «A quanto ha venduto il dipinto»?

8-18

1. «Vorrei del pane». «Quanto»?
2. «Ha comprato molti libri». «Sai quanti esattamente»?
3. «Ha sepolto cinque mogli». «Quante»?!
4. «Quanto costano quelle scarpe»?
5. «Quanto vuoi per quella barca»?
6. «Quanto costano quei guanti»?
7. «Quanto costa quel vestito»?
8. «Ecco il suo formaggio». «Quanto fa»?

8-19

1. Quanti ne prendete a prestito?
2. Quanta ne bevi ogni giorno?
3. Quanti ne invita?
4. Quanto ne volete?
5. Quanta ne compri?
6. Quante ne mandano?

8-20

1. «Gli piace molto il vino». «Quanto ne beve»?
2. «Vorrei delle arance». «Quante ne vuole, Signore»?
3. «Compro dieci computer». «Quanti ne compri»?!
4. «Sta imparando un'altra lingua straniera». «Quante ne parla»?
5. «Quanti anelli porta»? «Ne porta otto».

Unit 9

9-1

1. Il cane che hanno preso non abbaia mai.
2. La barca che lei vuole comprare è nuova.
3. I giocattoli che avete lasciato in giardino sono tutti bagnati.
4. Un vino che ci piace molto è il barbaresco.
5. L'architetto che progetta la loro nuova casa è giovane.

9-2

1. Conosci lo scienziato che parlerà stasera?
2. La relazione che Giulia sta scrivendo è molto importante.
3. Le mele che avete raccolto ieri sono molto buone.
4. Il terremoto che ha colpito la California era molto forte.
5. La ragazza che ho incontrato in vacanza è andata in Australia.
6. Nel 1908 Ford lanciò l'automobile Modello T, che costava novecentocinquanta dollari.
7. Gli operai che ha assunto per costruire la casa sono marocchini.

9-3

1. Il problema cui ti riferisci è stato risolto.
2. La persona cui pensavi per quel lavoro non è disponibile.
3. L'amica cui Carla si sente più vicina è mia sorella.
4. Il gatto cui si erano tanto affezionati è morto improvvisamente.
5. La conferenza cui abbiamo assistito ieri era interessante.
6. La parrocchia cui apparteniamo verrà chiusa.

9-4

1. A volte dico delle cose di cui poi mi pento.
2. Questo è l'amico di cui ti abbiamo parlato.
3. Ha sposato una cantante di cui hai sentito parlare.
4. La lettera di cui si sono dimenticati era molto importante.
5. Abbiamo discusso il progetto di cui sono responsabile.
6. Su quello scaffale troverai il materiale di cui hai bisogno.

9-5

1. La ragazza con cui gioco a tennis è una vecchia amica.
2. Il ragazzo con cui sta parlando è mio figlio.
3. Il candidato per cui ho votato non ha vinto le elezioni.
4. Il cassetto in cui hai messo le chiavi è vuoto.
5. La scrivania su cui hai lasciato le chiavi è stata pulita.
6. La signora per cui sta comprando un regalo è sua moglie.

9-6

1. La ragazza con la quale gioco a tennis è una vecchia amica.
2. Il ragazzo con il quale sta parlando è mio figlio
3. Il candidato per il quale ho votato non ha vinto le elezioni.
4. Il cassetto nel quale hai messo le chiavi è vuoto.
5. La scrivania sulla quale hai lasciato le chiavi è stata pulita.
6. La parrocchia alla quale apparteniamo è stata chiusa.

9-7

1. Gianni, la cui macchina è stata rubata, ha bisogno di un taxi.
2. Lo studente il cui tema ho letto ieri, scrive bene.
3. Lo studente la cui promozione stiamo festeggiando è il fratello di Maria.
4. Ada e Lia, di cui apprezzi l'intelligenza, studiano medicina.
5. Ha scritto un libro il cui titolo non ricordo.
6. Lo scienziato la cui scoperta era su tutti i giornali è morto improvvisamente.
7. La casa il cui tetto è crollato è stata costruita male.

9-8

1. Chi mi conosce bene si fida di me.
2. Chi passa il primo esame viene ammesso all'esame finale.
3. Chi gioca d'azzardo spesso perde.
4. Chi ha bisogno d'aiuto deve contattare un medico.
5. Chi ha letto quel libro lo considera un capolavoro.

9-9

1. Dimmi a chi devo mandare questo pacco.
2. Ho visto chi hanno invitato.
3. Volete sapere a chi vendono la loro casa?
4. Desideriamo ringraziare chi ci ha aiutato.
5. Non fidarti di chi fa troppe promesse.
6. Chi lo richiede riceverà il depliant.
7. Vuole sapere chi guadagna più di lei.

9-10

1. Mi ricorderò di quanto hai fatto per me.
2. Si rivolge a quanti hanno perso i loro soldi in quell'imbroglio.
3. Siamo molto spiacenti per quanto è successo.
4. Non aggiungerò nulla a quanto ho detto.
5. Ti restituisco quanto ti devo.
6. Quanto ci chiede non è molto.
7. Il giudice ha ordinato l'arresto di quanti hanno partecipato allo sciopero.

9-11

1. Ogni volta che fa un discorso mi addormento.
2. Il giorno che lei capirà i miei guai sarà un gran giorno.
3. L'abbiamo portato a visitare il paese dove erano vissuti i suoi genitori.
4. Conosci un negozio dove posso trovare dei sandali?
5. Non dimenticherà mai l'anno che suo fratello ebbe quell'incidente di macchina.
6. Elisa non sa più dove ha messo le chiavi delle macchina.
7. L'albergo dove abbiamo passato tante belle vacanze è stato chiuso.

Unit 10

10-1

1. Questo è il mio libro, quello è il tuo.
2. Prendi queste scarpe. Quelle non sono della tua misura.
3. Quelli sono i vostri posti.
4. Questa è la nostra nuova professoressa di matematica.
5. Quale vestito preferisci? Questo o quello?
6. Questa è mia moglie.
7. Vuoi queste?
8. I miei figli? Questi non sono i miei figli.

10-2

1. Non voglio parlare di quella là.
2. Guarda quello là, con quel buffo cappello in testa!
3. Ascolta questo qua; pensa di sapere tutto.
4. Compri questo qui?
5. Non abbiamo bisogno di questi qui. Sono inutili.
6. Pensa sempre a quelli là.
7. Con quella là non vai lontano.

10-3

1. Mi piace il vestito lungo, a lei piace quello corto.
2. Quale vuoi? Quello giallo o quello rosso?
3. Quella grande è ideale per la nostra famiglia.
4. Dammi la penna nera, non quella rossa.
5. Metti il bicchiere grande a sinistra, e quello piccolo a destra.
6. Mi piacciono i cani grossi; a lei piacciono quelli piccoli.

Unit 11

1. Queste scarpe non sono le tue, sono le mie.
2. La casa rosa è la loro.
3. Il mio gatto è affettuoso; il loro no.
4. La sua casa è grande come la vostra.
5. La mia penna? No, questa è la tua.
6. La mia macchina fotografica è qui; la sua è sullo scaffale.
7. I tuoi sci sono pronti, i suoi no.

1. Your book has had great success; hers hasn't.
2. We sold our boat. Now we use his.
3. The blue hat is not yours. It's his.
4. Take the yellow gloves; the red ones are hers.
5. "Did they see your daughters at the party?" "No, but they saw his."

1. La sua casa è più piccola della mia.
2. Non mi interessa la sua proposta, ma mi interessa la tua.
3. Pensi sempre ai suoi problemi, mai ai miei!
4. I nostri interessi contrastano con i loro.
5. Ecco i cappotti. Prendi il tuo.
6. Si occupano delle mie tasse, o delle sue?
7. Non comprare la loro casa; compra la sua.
8. Abbiamo investito nel suo fondo, non nel vostro.

11-4

1. Quel poliziotto è uno dei nostri amici.
2. Sta parlando con uno dei suoi insegnanti.
3. Uno dei loro gatti si è perso.
4. Due dei suoi colleghi parlano cinese.
5. Possiamo prendere una delle tue macchine?
6. Una delle mie figlie vive in Australia.
7. Lavoro con uno dei vostri cugini.

11-5

1. Il suo computer è più veloce del mio.
2. Quella bici è la sua, non questa.
3. Il tuo lavoro è interessante quanto il suo.
4. Quale gonna è la mia? Quella blu.
5. Non prendere quell'impermeabile. È il suo.
6. Il nostro progetto è migliore del vostro.
7. Questo è il nostro indirizzo. Volete anche il loro?

Unit 12

1. No one wants fish.
2. Each believes what he/she wants.
3. Both went skiing.
4. Each is happy with what he has.
5. Everyone is happy.
6. Someone is looking for you.
7. The door was open. Anyone could have stolen the radio.
8. Franca saw no one.
9. "Do you want any oranges?" "I'd like some."
10. They no longer talk with one another.
11. I don't like this skirt. Can I try on another?

1. Viene qualcuno?
2. Nessuno va con loro.
3. Invito tutti e due alla festa.
4. C'è qualcuno al telefono per te.
5. Chiunque saprebbe scrivere quel romanzo.

12-3

1. Invito tutti i miei amici, ma solo alcuni vengono.
2. Nessuno è pronto per il viaggio.
3. Parli con qualcuno?
4. Ti ricordi di tutti?
5. Chiunque vorrebbe quella casa.
6. Siete tutti pronti?
7. «Non inviti nessuno»? «No, non invito nessuno».
8. Nessuno dei due vuole rispondere alla tua domanda.
9. Tutti e due rispondono bene alle mie domande.

12-4

1. Sono in tanti a venire alla mia festa.
2. Sono venuti in tanti a salutare mio zio.
3. Sono in molti a volerla sposare.
4. Sono in tanti a volerla sposare.

12-5

1. Ha cercato una scusa per il suo comportamento, ma non ne ha trovata nessuna.
2. Non hanno trovato nessuno.
3. Ognuno ha il diritto di esprimere la propria opinione.
4. «Vuoi delle pesche»? «Dammene solo qualcuna».
5. «Abbiamo molti fichi. Ne vuoi qualcuno»? «No, grazie».
6. Non c'era nessuno in giro.
7. Sono rimasti tutti scioccati quando hanno sentito la notizia.

12-6

1. Many of you forgot to sign.
2. There is nothing important in that message.
3. Several of my friends don't speak English.
4. Nothing of what you're saying makes sense.
5. Umberto never did anything good in his life.
6. Something in her doesn't convince me.
7. I like everything about her.
8. Much of what you've done has been useless.

12-7

1. Uno di voi ha rubato il quadro.
2. Ciascuna delle candidate ha superato l'esame.
3. Alcuni di noi sono d'accordo con te.
4. Il direttore ha parlato con ciascuno di noi.
5. Non parla con nessuno di loro.

12-8

1. Non vogliono niente.
2. Vuole qualcosa da me.
3. Non funziona niente qui.
4. Non mangiate mai niente.
5. Non mangia niente.
6. È andato tutto bene.
7. Non fare nient' altro.

12-9

1. Did you prepare everything?
2. She didn't see anything.
3. They are looking for something to give her.
4. "It's late, but do you want anything to eat?" "No, thanks."
5. "You must be hungry! Do you want something to eat?" "Yes, please."
6. We found nothing beautiful in that store.
7. Is he saying something new?
8. Would you like (*desiderare, pres. simple*) something else, Madam?
9. I can't do anything else for him.

12-10

1. Non darmi tanto vino. Ne voglio solo un po'.
2. «Beve molto vino»? «No, ne beve poco».
3. Vuoi un po' di cognac?
4. Non mangi troppo?
5. «Abbiamo abbastanza formaggio per la festa»? «Ne abbiamo anche troppo».

Unit 13

13-1

1. Non tirare la coda al gatto.
2. Ho messo la biancheria nella lavatrice.
3. Appendiamo il quadro nello studio.
4. Sul colle c'era la neve.
5. Dove sono i giocattoli dei bambini?
6. Andranno alla sua festa domani sera.
7. L'esplorazione dello spazio incominciò negli anni cinquanta del XX secolo.
8. Dalla finestra si vede il mare.
9. Ha piantato delle viti sulla collina.
10. Hai parlato col dottore?
11. Non ha ereditato niente dai suoi genitori.
12. Le chiavi non sono nel cassetto.
13. Hai parlato agli zii delle vacanze?
14. Negli scavi hanno trovato una tomba ricchissima.
15. La luce delle stelle è fortissima in cima ai monti.
16. Non ha messo la data sugli assegni.
17. Avete cercato nelle tasche?
18. *Dagli Appennini alle Ande* è un romanzo per ragazzi.
19. Non aspettatevi molto dal negoziato.
20. Abbiamo riflettuto a lungo sulle sue parole.
21. All'hotel non c'era nessuno.
22. Guarda tutti dall'alto in basso.
23. Non ci piace la torta all'arancia.
24. C'era la disperazione nei suoi occhi.
25. Il motore a scoppio fun inventato nell'Ottocento.
26. Hai bisogno della macchina?
27. Usa ancora i libri scolastici dell'anno scorso.
28. Non è amato molto dalle sue sorelle.
29. Non fidarti degli estranei.
30. Non ricordo il titolo del libro.
31. Collo sforzo che hai fatto, meriti un premio.
32. I soldati uscirono allo scoperto.
33. Ai miei tempi si andava a piedi.
34. Ho messo la picozza sullo zaino.
35. Hanno messo tante luci sui tetti delle case!
36. Ha fatto quella foto coll'obiettivo sbagliato.
37. Sull'orizzonte si vedeva una sottile linea rossa.
38. Il coniglio venne catturato dall'aquila.
39. La serratura dell'armadio è rotta.
40. Colla fortuna che ho, perderò il treno.
41. Hanno parlato coi guardiani del magazzino.
42. Era stremata dallo sforzo.
43. Sono coll'acqua alla gola.
44. Abbiamo messo dei fiori freschi sull'altare.
45. L'aereo finì nell'occhio del ciclone.
46. Non parla più cogli zii.
47. Giochi ancora colle tue cugine?

13-2

1. The horse is inside the corral.
2. She hid behind the house.
3. The airplane is flying over the valley.
4. A lot of insects live underground.
5. We'll stop by at your place after dinner.
6. Except for Massimo, we all agree.
7. Hannibal entered Italy through the Little Saint Bernard Pass.
8. In my opinion, he is right.
9. They left for the Amazon despite our warnings.
10. Are you all against Paola?
11. They don't eat meat during Lent.

13-3

1. I did it for my sister's sake.
2. Gianni cannot live without her.
3. We got the loan thanks to you.
4. Mario got the job instead of Michele.
5. Because of our lawyer's mistakes, we lost the lawsuit.
6. No one ever came into this valley before we did.
7. My mother is sad because we all live far away from her.
8. May I sit close to you?
9. I would go to the top of Mount Everest with him.

13-4

1. I'm going skiing on Sunday.
2. Are you going to Maria's to study?
3. Tell her not to buy milk.
4. They tried to warn them.
5. They're going to the airport to pick her up.
6. We need some help to finish this job.
7. Give me a book to read.
8. They scolded him because he made too much noise.

Unit 14

14-1

1. Maria's cat
2. the cat's tail
3. last week's newspaper
4. the peach tree
5. U.N. officials
6. a fifteen-year-old boy
7. a three-hundred-page book
8. the wood table

14-2
1. Scrive un libro di due volumi.
2. Ha una ragazza di dieci anni.
3. Non vuole un tavolo di marmo.
4. Non riusciamo a trovare il cane di Maria.
5. Hanno evacuato tutti i funzionari delle Nazioni Unite.
6. La coda del gatto è bianca e nera.
7. Leggi i giornali del mese scorso?
8. Vogliamo piantare cinque alberi di mele.

14-3
1. Do you want to see yesterday's newspaper?
2. We have to write a thirty-page essay.
3. I want to install a wool carpet.
4. The departure of the group has been set for 9 A.M.
5. He writes French books.
6. That closet is full of old clothes.
7. Giulia's dog died.

14-4
1. Indagano sul suo ruolo nella crisi finanziaria della ditta.
2. Non ho notizie circa la malattia di sua madre, Signor Pertini.
3. Farà quel film sulla rivoluzione francese?
4. Non so niente riguardo alla sua richiesta, Signore.
5. Siamo partiti tutti, con l'eccezione di Antonella.
6. Mario non mi ha più detto niente circa quell'affare.
7. Scrivi libri sulla letteratura russa.

14-5
1. Alcuni degli studenti hanno protestato.
2. Ci sono dei criminali tra i suoi amici.
3. È la più intelligente di tutti.
4. Alcuni membri della squadra si rifiutano di giocare.
5. Alcuni di voi voteranno per il nuovo candidato.
6. C'è un medico tra i passeggeri?

14-6
1. Vado in montagna con delle guide esperte.
2. Avete preso contatto con degli avvocati?
3. Stavo parlando di alcune conoscenze che ho incontrato a teatro.
4. Ha visto un documentario su dei pesci strani.
5. Ho pensato a delle soluzioni al tuo problema.
6. Siamo passati per delle valli selvagge.
7. Si sono dimenticati di alcuni appuntamenti.
8. Ho comprato questi regali per delle mie cugine.

14-7
1. I hope I'll see them again soon.
2. We were thinking of stopping by Maria's place.
3. Elena decided to emigrate to Australia.
4. You forgot to close the garage again!
5. I have no intention of following his advice.
6. Riccardo doesn't care at all about us.
7. Her grandmother looked after her after her parents' death.
8. Don't you trust us?
9. They don't need to sell their stocks any longer.
10. Giancarlo doesn't want to do his homework.
11. We are thinking of opening a store.

Unit 15

15-1
1. Gli uccelli migrano a sud in autunno.
2. Hanno una bella casa nelle Prealpi venete.
3. Hanno fatto il trasloco a Parigi.
4. Si è fatto una casetta in montagna.
5. Non le piace vivere in città.
6. Ha vissuto nei paesi più strani.
7. Voliamo a Praga domani.
8. Facciamo un viaggio in Cina.
9. Hanno passato due mesi nella Cina meridionale.
10. A nord c'è la stella polare.
11. Passeranno il Natale in India.
12. Hanno comprato una villetta in periferia.

15-2
1. Volo a Londra domani.
2. Vanno in campagna ogni fine settimana.
3. Passano tutte le estati al mare.
4. Loro vivono in città, noi, invece, viviamo in campagna.
5. Non puoi andare in macchina a San Pietro.
6. Ci vediamo a Vienna?
7. Si trasferisce in New Mexico.
8. Mi trasferisco in centro.
9. Vi piace la vita in provincia?

15-3

1. The children went into Dad's study.
2. Don't put your shoes on the sofa!
3. The two teams entered the stadium.
4. We are on the soccer field, ready to play.
5. They didn't all get on the bus.
6. The cardinal celebrated the state funeral in the cathedral.
7. We were the only ones on the summit.
8. Look how many sailing boats are out at sea today!

15-4

1. Hai lasciato la pentola sul gas.
2. In quella stanza ci sono solo due letti.
3. Posso mettere le mie maglie in quell'armadio?
4. È ora di risalire sull'autobus.
5. Ci sono solo sei patate nella pentola.
6. Hai dei soldi nel portafoglio?
7. Le due squadre entrano nello stadio.
8. C'è posto per otto sulla barca?

15-5

1. Il cappello è sulla sua testa.
2. Jules Verne è l'autore di *Ventimila leghe sotto i mari*.
3. Il lampadario è appeso sopra il tavolo.
4. Ha messo una lampada alogena sulla scrivania.
5. La gatta si è nascosta sotto il letto.
6. Sono stati sul Monte Everest.
7. Non le piace andare sott'acqua.
8. Viviamo all'ultimo piano. Non vogliamo avere nessuno sopra di noi.

15-6

1. We stayed home the entire weekend.
2. Elisabetta has not been going to church since she was fifteen.
3. "Where is Pietro?" "He went to the bakery."
4. You will find him at work, Mr. Cellini.
5. Sister Chiara is at the parish.
6. I do have to go to the bank. I have no money left.
7. How long were you in the hospital?
8. They spend the entire summer in their backyard (garden).
9. I kept my son at home this morning. He had a temperature.
10. Are you coming to the theater with us tomorrow evening?
11. It's incredible. My daughter has fun in school.
12. Shall we meet in the square?

15-7

1. Luisa è andata a teatro con sua madre.
2. Non voglio andare in ospedale!
3. Ha passato il sabato pomeriggio in chiesa a pulire i banchi.
4. Mia figlia è andata in banca da sola per la prima volta.
5. Lo sai che non puoi portare i criceti a scuola.
6. Stia attento, sa, che la trascino in tribunale!
7. È una settimana che sono chiusa in casa con l'influenza.
8. L'avvocato non è in studio, oggi.
9. Ai bambini fa bene andare in piscina.
10. Preferisci stare in hotel o in campeggio?
11. In cartoleria adesso vendono anche i giornali.

15-8

1. L'ho visto dal tabaccaio.
2. Passiamo la domenica pomeriggio da me o da te?
3. Non si può più andare da quel lattaio. Non ha mai il latte fresco.
4. Sono passata dall'infermiera a fare il vaccino antiinfluenzale.
5. Il prezzo della carne è salito alle stelle dal nostro macellaio.
6. Mia sorella ha portato sua figlia Nicoletta dal pediatra.
7. Non va più dal barbiere perché ha deciso di lasciarsi crescere i capelli.
8. Sono dal notaio per la lettura del testamento.

15-9

1. Shall we take the children to the playground?
2. He is not at home. He is on campus.
3. They spend their Saturday afternoons at the shopping mall.
4. Passengers are kindly requested to go to gate number 8.
5. There was a long line at passport control.
6. We always have lunch at the fast-food place.
7. Is there anything interesting at the movies?

15-10
1. Venite anche voi allo stadio?
2. Non arriveremo mai all'aeroporto con questo traffico!
3. Per fortuna, l'ambulanza è arrivata all'ospedale in tempo.
4. Dobbiamo essere al terminal alle sei di mattina.
5. Alla stazione dei taxi non c'era neanche una macchina!
6. Lasciate i bambini tutti il pomeriggio al doposcuola?
7. I dimostranti si erano piazzati all'ingresso della sala dei congressi.

15-11
1. Ho prenotato una visita dal medico.
2. Si sono visti a casa di mia cugina.
3. Si sono visti da mia cugina.
4. Ha passato la notte in biblioteca a studiare per l'esame.
5. Non le piace vivere al decimo piano. Soffre di acrofobia.
6. Sulla luna non c'è acqua.
7. Mangiano almeno una volta la settimana in pizzeria.
8. Quanti passeggeri c'erano sulla nave che è affondata?
9. Andiamo dall'avvocato per parlare del divorzio.
10. Ci vediamo al bar alle due?
11. Il cane non è stato fermo un momento dal veterinario.
12. I bambini si sono nascosti in camera da letto.
13. Non mette mai la macchina in garage.
14. Ha piantato tre peri in giardino.
15. Si è chiusa in casa tre mesi fa e non ne è più uscita.

15-12
1. Our neighbor spends the entire day looking out the window.
2. Did you take down that ugly painting from the wall?
3. His father was from a well-off family.
4. I have to take a pebble out of my shoe.
5. Have you noticed that she took her wedding ring off her finger?
6. Stop thinking about those crazy ideas!
7. They live two blocks away from us.
8. Keep away from the gate. That dog is dangerous.
9. Keep your hands off the doors.

15-13
1. Partiamo dall'aeroporto della Malpensa.
2. Non siamo più molto lontani dalla vetta.
3. Sei di origine scozzese?
4. La polizia cercò di fare allontanare gli ostaggi dalla finestra.
5. Avete preso un numero per la lotteria dal sacchetto?
6. Il mago estrasse la carta giusta dal mazzo.
7. Si sono trasferiti a duecento metri dai loro genitori.
8. Il suo fidanzato è di famiglia nobile.
9. L'italiano deriva dal latino.
10. Ha copiato tutto il compito di matematica dal suo vicino di banco.

15-14
1. Luigi will be back from the university after 8 P.M.
2. Are you coming from your brother's place?
3. I'm going to my brother's for dinner.
4. Look, Dad is coming from the drugstore with your medication.
5. I no longer want to go to that dentist.
6. I have to go back to the dentist because the tooth is still aching.
7. He can't talk because he has just come back from the dentist.

15-15
1. La nuova casa si trova tra Genova e Livorno.
2. Sono passati dal paese.
3. Mettete la crema pasticcera tra due strati di sfoglia.
4. Ho viaggiato per tutta l'Europa.
5. L'ospite d'onore passa dalla porta principale.
6. I rapitori passarono per i boschi.

15-16
1. C'erano cinquanta giornalisti fuori dal tribunale.
2. Abbiamo passeggiato lungo il fiume.
3. Vivono lontano dalla loro famiglia.
4. C'è un fioraio dall'altra parte della strada.
5. Siediti vicino a me.
6. Era in piedi vicino alla finestra.
7. Nessuno si era mai avventurato oltre le montagne.
8. Gli uccelli erano tutti intorno al lago.

Unit 16

16-1
1. It was cold at Easter.
2. I saw him the last time in 1999.
3. We go skiing in winter.
4. They got married in May.
5. At what time are you leaving?
6. *and* 7. In August it is very hot.
8. They ought to be here already by now.
9. Marco always came to visit in the evening.

16-2
1. Tutti si travestono a Carnevale.
2. Le lezioni incominciano alle otto.
3. Le violette fioriscono in/a marzo.
4. La prima guerra mondiale scoppiò nel 1914.
5. Nacque in una bella giornata di primavera.
6. Ha telefonato al medico alle tre di mattina.
7. Di domenica si va a messa.
8. Va a fare la spesa di pomeriggio.

16-3
1. Il treno parte alle 10:30.
2. Sofia è arrivata di notte.
3. Vuoi fare quel viaggio a/in settembre?
4. Kennedy fu eletto presidente nel 1960.
5. È bello andare a pescare in una calda giornata d'estate.
6. A Ferragosto tutti i negozi sono chiusi.
7. È nato nel XIX secolo!
8. I dinosauri vissero nel quaternario.

16-4
1. We're going horseback riding next weekend.
2. Are you free this morning?
3. They stayed at our place all day.
4. I'll get back to work (on) Tuesday.
5. The twins were born in 1985, (on) August 10th.
6. We'll meet again one day.
7. What will you do next Saturday?
8. I went to the beach last week.

16-5
1. Passerò da te sabato.
2. Passa da lei tutti i sabati.
3. È nato di lunedì.
4. Vanno a ginnastica il martedì.
5. Partiremo per la Nuova Zelanda in novembre, non so ancora il giorno.
6. Vi siete divertiti a Capodanno?
7. Siete arrivati a un'ora impossibile. Ma dove siete stati?
8. Non si semina l'insalata a gennaio!
9. È nato il 15 maggio.
10. Sono morti tutti nel 1998, in quel terribile incidente.

16-6
1. Lavoro dalle nove alle cinque.
2. La conosco da gennaio.
3. La casa è vuota da marzo.
4. Nicola esce con Paola da dieci anni.
5. Vendiamo caldaie dal 1925.
6. Il dottore sarà libero dalle quattro (in poi).
7. Da lunedì (in poi), il negozio chiuderà alle ventuno.
8. La conosco dall'infanzia.

16-7

1. Elisa ha studiato (per) tutta la notte.
2. Elisa studierà solo anatomia per due settimane.
3. Ho lavorato con Paolo per cinque anni.
4. Lavora con mia sorella quattro ore al giorno.
5. Lavorerà con mia sorella per quattro ore.
6. Mia madre ha studiato il pianoforte per dieci anni.
7. Sua zia ha studiato l'inglese per tre anni.
8. Studierà l'inglese per sei mesi in Australia.

16-8

1. Non ci parliamo più da mesi.
2. Non gli ho parlato per dei mesi.
3. Non gli parlo dalla notte di Capodanno del 2000.
4. Irma parla con Angelo al telefono un'ora ogni giorno.
5. Resteremo negli Stati Uniti (per) cinque anni.
6. Si è presa cura di suo marito per cinque anni.
7. Siamo sposati da dieci anni.
8. Sono proprio stanca. Andiamo in vacanza (per) una settimana?
9. Siamo stati sposati (per) dieci anni.
10. Non la vedo da lunedì.

16-9

1. Partiamo entro giovedì.
2. Partiamo giovedì.
3. Torna tra due anni?
4. Lo sposerà entro la fine dell'anno.
5. Lo sposerà entro il 20 dicembre.
6. Saranno divorziati entro/tra un anno.
7. Sarò a casa entro le cinque.
8. «Posso prendere la tua macchina»? «Sì ma devo averla indietro entro stasera».

16-10

1. I'll call you before my departure.
2. I'll see you after lunch.
3. You'll get it before the end of the day.
4. Luca will arrive after sunset.
5. They put off the discussion until after dinner.
6. Please, after you, Madam.
7. Are you coming back before tomorrow?
8. They disappeared one after the other.
9. You are ahead of me.
10. After you, no one will take care of the garden.

Unit 17

17-1

1. He gave chocolates to his aunt.
2. Did you mail your application to the admissions office at the university?
3. I gave him all my money. He will invest it for me.
4. Did you buy milk for the cat?
5. They delivered a package for your father.
6. They delivered a package to your father.
7. They sent him a package.
8. We told the truth to Lucia.
9. Ask Robert.
10. He fought for his country's freedom.

17-2

1. Ha fatto grandi sacrifici per i suoi figli.
2. In quel museo puoi vedere dei vecchi macchinari per la produzione della seta.
3. Le abbiamo regalato i gioielli di mia madre.
4. Hanno dato i gioielli di mia madre a lei e non a me.
5. Fanno molto lavoro volontario per i bambini orfani.
6. «Ti interessa la speleologia»? «No, non mi interessa».
7. L'ONU accetta contributi per le vittime dello tsunami.
8. Che cosa hai fatto ai tuoi vestiti?

17-3

1. Gianna is taking ski lessons with her cousin.
2. My dog plays all the time (together) with her cat.
3. Sandra has made an appointment with her doctor.
4. Federico shows up every evening at the bar accompanied by a strange guy.
5. We'll go on a trip together with some old friends of ours.
6. With whom are you going out for dinner?
7. It's impossible to talk with you.

17-4

1. Si è fidanzato con una giapponese.
2. Mio figlio dorme ancora con l'orsacchiotto di peluche.
3. Nadia viene dalla pettrinatice con te.
4. Se lavori insieme a tuo fratello, gli affari andranno meglio.
5. Con lui sono sempre a mio agio.
6. Vedo sempre Francesca in compagnia del suo professore d'università.
7. Quella vecchia signora vive con trenta gatti.

17-5

1. Sono stato intervistato da tre registi.
2. La mia automobile è stata danneggiata da un ramo.
3. Non era amata dai suoi figli.
4. L'hotel è stato sepolto dalla valanga.
5. La Gallia fu conquistata da Giulio Cesare.
6. Il latte è stato versato dal gatto.
7. Renato è stato morso da un serpente.

17-6

1. Do you want something to eat?
2. I've got a lot to do.
3. I've got nothing to do.
4. Could you give me something to drink?
5. That's a film worth seeing.
6. I have dinner to prepare.
7. My grandfather doesn't have much time to live.

17-7

1. Che cos'hai da fare?
2. Il rapinatore aveva molti crimini da confessare.
3. Il poliziotto ha tre casi da risolvere.
4. Non hanno niente da dirsi.
5. Quella camicetta è da lavare.
6. Dopo tante discussioni, il ponte è ancora da costruire.
7. Tre appartamenti sono ancora da vendere.

Unit 18

18-1

1. Andiamo a Mosca in treno.
2. Vado a lavorare in bici.
3. Viaggia sempre in aereo.
4. È meglio andare a Milano in treno o in macchina?
5. Hanno attraversato l'Oceano Atlantico in barca.
6. I ribelli scapparono in elicottero.
7. Faremo il giro del mondo in nave.
8. Girate per la campagna in moto?

18-2

1. My mother cleaned the rug with vinegar.
2. What stocks did you buy with your wife's money?
3. Anna covered her head with a scarf.
4. My cat is playing with the curtain rods.
5. You won't be able to take down that tree with this saw.
6. You won't go far by bike.
7. We'll get downtown faster by subway.
8. They announced the end of the war with a radio message.

18-3

1. Vai da Londra a Roma con il treno?
2. Con l'eredtà di mio nonno compro una casetta sul mare.
3. I nomadi attraversavano il deserto con i cammelli.
4. Risponderò alle vostre domande con una lettera.
5. A Silvia piace la pasta con il burro e il parmigiano.
6. È una spremuta fatta con le arance del suo frutteto.
7. Troia fu presa con un cavallo finto.
8. Gli piace girare per la campagna con la moto.

18-4
1. They prefer to travel with a rental car.
2. Ada is leaving with the 9 P.M. plane.
3. Massimo will come with his new motorbike.
4. They sailed around the world with the boat that won the America's Cup.
5. Do you want to travel to China with that truck?!
6. I do thirty kilometers an hour with that racing bike.

18-5
1. Volo a New York con l'aereo delle diciassette.
2. Isabella va a fare la spesa con la Rolls-Royce di suo padre.
3. Vuoi andare sul Monte McKinley con la tua mountain bike?
4. Mio fratello va in giro per il paese con il suo nuovo Hummer.
5. Con il treno delle otto arriveremo a Manhattan alle 10:30.
6. Mandano gli astronauti sulla luna con un vecchio razzo.

18-6
1. D'estate vado a lavorare in [con la] bici.
2. Con questa nave spaziale non arriveremo mai su Arturo.
3. Siamo andati in Russia in [con la] moto.
4. Ha vinto la corsa con la moto di suo zio.
5. Voglio attraversare l'Alaska in [con il] treno.
6. La Vasaloppet è una gara che si fa con gli sci da fondo.
7. Ha attraversato la Siberia d'inverno in [con la] slitta.
8. Riuscite a fare cinquanta chilometri al giorno in bici?

18-7
1. Gli ecologisti sono contrari alle centrali a carbone perché sono molto inquinanti.
2. Il pianoforte è uno strumento a percussione; il clavicembalo è uno strumento a corda.
3. Stiamo riscoprendo i mulini a vento, perché usano una fonte di energia rinnovabile.
4. Le barche a vela italiane non hanno moi vinto America's Cup.
5. Finalmente mi sono liberata della cucina elettrica e ne ho installata una a gas.

18-8
1. Non gli piace il computer. Usa ancora una vecchia macchina da scrivere manuale!
2. Stasera mangiamo solo il secondo e il dolce. Non c'è bisogno dei piatti da minestra.
3. Vince sempre a poker perché usa carte da gioco truccate.
4. Non andare sul ghiacciaio senza gli occhiali da sole, può farti male agli occhi.
5. Da bambimi avevamo un cane da caccia , perchè mio padre era un grande cacciatore.
6. Vuoi una mountain bike o una bicicletta da corsa?
7. Per l'ingresso in società della figlia daranno una festa da ballo con trecento invitati.
8. Sono andata al mare senza il costume da bagno, così ho nuotato nuda.
9. Carlo insiste a giocare a golf, ma perde sempre le palline da golf nel bosco.
10. Ho dato il mio biglietto da visita al direttore della banca. Spero che mi dia un lavoro.

18-9
1. Mio marito ha dipinto tutta la casa, ma l'ha fatto proprio di malavoglia.
2. È arrivata di corsa perchè pensava di essere in ritardo.
3. Mangia di magro per dimagrire.
4. Ti vesti sempre di rosso?
5. Non posso parlarti adesso. Sono di fretta/di corsa.

18-10
1. Non dipinge più a olio, solo ad acquerello.
2. Ettore parla sempre a voce bassa, non capisco mai niente.
3. Queste scarpe costano un sacco di soldi perché sono fatte a mano.
4. Siete pregati di compilare il modulo scrivendo a stampatello.
5. Nessuno dei corsi mi interessa particolarmente, così ho scelto a caso.
6. Ha imparato tutte le tragedie di Shakespeare a memoria.
7. Comprano tutto a credito. Uno di questi giorni faranno bancarotta.
8. I prezzi all'ingrosso sono stabili, ma al mercato quelli al minuto sono saliti del 3 percento in un mese.

18-11

1. Il podologo dice che le scarpe a punta danneggiano le dita dei piedi.
2. Mio nonno passa tutte le sue serate seduto davanti al fuoco sulla sua sedia a dondolo.
3. In quel collegio alle bambine non lasciano portare i pantaloni, solo le gonne a pieghe.
4. Portava un cappello a larghe tese che gli nascondeva quasi tutto il viso.
5. Mi piacciono molto i pantaloni alla pescatora, che erano di moda negli anni cinquanta.

18-12

1. Con me il Signor Calandri si è sempre comportato da galantuomo.
2. Ho visto un uomo dall'aria sospetta dietro casa e ho chiamato la polizia.
3. Sandro, non mettere le scarpe sul tavolo! Comportati da persona educata.
4. C'era una ragazza dai capelli biondi, ma non era Vittoria.
5. Non ci ho guadagnato niente a trattarti da amico.

18-13

1. Fai le cose con calma, abbiamo tutto il tempo necessario.
2. Hai agito con cautela non investendo i soldi in quell'affare.
3. Ti sei comportata con leggerezza parlando in pubblico degli affari del tuo cliente.
4. Abbiamo una perdita nel tetto, la macchina è rotta e mio figlio ha perso le chiavi di casa, ma noi prendiamo tutto con senso dell'umorismo.
5. Ti auguro con tutto il cuore di trovare la persona giusta per te.
6. Abbiamo fatto le cose con cura, eppure ci sono ancora degli errori.
7. Sono arrivati col fiato corto, ma almeno sono riusciti a non perdere il treno.

18-14

1. Al matrimonio c'erano almeno tre signore in bianco come la sposa.
2. Marianna è in dubbio/in forse se accettare quel lavoro o no.
3. Bambini, non potete camminare tutti insieme, mettetevi in fila indiana.
4. Ci siamo fatti tutti in quattro a dare una mano, quando c'è stata l'alluvione.
5. Ti ringrazio di aver messo tutte quelle cartelline in ordine alfabetico. C'era una tale confusione!
6. Lascia in pace tua sorella, non vedi che ha tanti compiti da fare?
7. Mangia in bianco da una vita, per quello è così magro.
8. In quel ristorante non accettano carte di credito o assegni; si paga solo in contanti.
9. Il vestito che costava trecento euro adesso ne costa solo centocinquanta perché è in saldo.

18-15

1. Ma dai, non prendertela, l'ho detto per scherzo!
2. Mi ha creduto sulla parola e mi ha dato il prestito.
3. Il mio avvocato ha voluto che mettessimo tutto per scritto.
4. Suo zio non ha mai comprato un abito fatto in vita sua. Si fa fare tutto su misura.
5. Le due amichette si chiusero in camera e si raccontarono tutto per filo e per segno.
6. Il testimone è ateo. Si rifiuta di giurare sulla Bibbia.
7. L'ho chiamato per nome, ma ha fatto finta di non conoscermi.

18-16

1. I senatori dell'opposizione voteranno a favore della legge contro il fumo.
2. I dissidenti hanno ottenuto asilo politico grazie all'intervento dell'ONU.
3. Abbiamo perso tutti i soldi per colpa di un consulente finanziario disonesto.
4. A causa della pioggia abbiamo dovuto rimandare la gita.
5. Non hanno divorziato per il bene dei loro figli.